mary-kate olsen   ashley olsen

ourstory

Mary-Kate and Ashley Olsen's Official Biography

As told to Damon Romine

HarperCollins*Entertainment*
An Imprint of HarperCollinsPublishers

A PARACHUTE PRESS BOOK

A PARACHUTE PRESS BOOK
Parachute Publishing, LLC
156 Fifth Avenue
Suite 302
New York, NY 10010

First published in the USA by HarperEntertainment 2003
Hardback edition first published in Great Britain by
HarperCollins*Entertainment* 2003
This paperback edition first published in Great Britain by
HarperCollins*Entertainment* 2004

HarperCollins *Entertainment* is an imprint of HarperCollins*Publishers* Ltd,
77-85 Fulham Palace Road, Hammersmith, London W6 8JB

Created and produced by Parachute Publishing LLC, in cooperation with
Dualstar Publications, a divison of Dualstar Entertainment Group, LLC.

Cover photograph courtesy of Dualstar Entertainment Group LLC
© Dualstar Entertainment Group LLC. 2003

The HarperCollins website address is
www.harpercollinschildrenbooks.co.uk

1 3 5 7 9 10 8 6 4 2

The author asserts the moral right to be identified as the author of the work.

ISBN 0 00 717545 0

Printed and bound in the UK by Bookmarque Ltd

Chapter 1

The Real Mary-Kate and Ashley

You and your friends are watching the MTV Video Music Awards on television, talking about the newest music and admiring the cool outfits the celebrities are wearing.

Then you spot your favourite stars stepping out of a limo at the end of a red carpet. You grew up watching them on television and in movies. You hold your breath as they wave to the crowd and smile into the camera.

It's Mary-Kate and Ashley Olsen. They have the life of big stars, you think. They're always so glamorous, always going to the hottest parties in Hollywood, right? Their lives seem so different from yours. But if you told that to Mary-Kate and

1

Ashley, they would most definitely disagree!

"Most of the time we do what every other teen does," Mary-Kate says.

"Right," Ashley agrees. "We go to school, hang with our friends, and go out on dates. You know, everyday stuff."

They take shopping trips to the local boutiques, rush out to catch the latest movies, and go to the beach. They're into kickboxing, yoga and Pilates.

"When we were younger we liked to kick around a soccer ball and we were cheerleaders. But now we're into going to the gym," Ashley says.

The sisters have crushes on celebrities and guys at school just like you do. They listen to the music of Dave Matthews, U2, John Mayer, and go to concerts with their friends.

It may be hard to believe but Mary-Kate and Ashley lead a very normal life. They were born on June 13, 1986. (Ashley is the older twin by two minutes!) They've grown up in suburban Los Angeles with their brother, Trent, who is two years older than they are, and their little sister, Elizabeth, who is three years younger. Their parents are divorced, and Mary-Kate and Ashley divide their time between living with their dad and with their mom. Their dad, Dave, is a mortgage broker. Their mom,

Jarnette (Jarnie), used to dance with the Los Angeles Ballet.

"Trent is a typical big brother," Mary-Kate says. "He thinks of us as his little sisters. He's very protective, but he also likes to tease us. He's great at drawing and sports. He's also into volleyball."

"We miss having him around all the time, now that he's in college," Ashley adds. "But luckily he's not that far away, and he tries to come home and have dinner as often as possible."

Lizzie, their younger sister, is very independent and well rounded. She loves ballet and acting. She has made a few guest appearances in some of Mary-Kate and Ashley's videos. Right now she's not interested in becoming a professional actress, but she enjoys performing in community theatre.

Mary-Kate and Ashley also have a sister and brother from their dad's second marriage to McKenzie Olsen. Taylor is six years old, and Jake is five. "It's great having little kids to play with," Ashley says. "We help out with baby-sitting a lot. With so many kids around, the house gets really crazy sometimes. But we love it!"

"Our family is a lot like everyone else's," says Mary-Kate. "Sometimes we argue. You know how it goes: one minute everyone is watching TV. The next, an argument breaks out over the remote control. But most of the time we get along great. We're very close, and we look out for each other. We all share our stuff. But the rule is you have to ask before borrowing something!"

"Mary-Kate could be a bit sneaky about 'borrowing' when she was little," reveals her mom, Jarnie. "Once, when the twins were very young, money was missing from all the kids' piggy banks."

"And suddenly Mary-Kate was very wealthy," adds their dad, Dave. "We divided the money back up and returned it to the correct piggy banks. Then Mary-Kate was benched for a while."

The Olsen household has always been filled with pets. They have had dogs, cats, birds, turtles and hamsters. Mary-Kate recently adopted a new puppy, a black Chihuahua-poodle mix that she named Jack – plus she and Ashley have two other dogs at their dad's house. Mary-Kate also has two horses, CD and Star. She stables them at a nearby ranch.

Horseback riding is one of Mary-Kate's favourite activities. "I love it. I'd go for a riding lesson every day if I could," she says. Mary-Kate has even competed in horse shows – and has the ribbons and trophies to prove it!

The Real Mary-Kate and Ashley

While Mary-Kate is riding, Ashley keeps busy with dance class, tennis and, most recently, golf. Her love of dance is something she inherited from her mother. Together the girls go to yoga class, which is great mental and physical exercise.

Both girls have very close friends whom they see all the time. They each have their own special friends, of course, but they also have good friends in common. When they were younger, Mary-Kate and Ashley and their friends would go Rollerblading, to Disneyland, or to a nearby amusement park called Knott's Berry Farm. "I remember how happy I was when we were finally tall enough to get on all the rides," says Ashley. "We'd ride every roller coaster there was!"

Once the girls took some of their friends to an amusement park to film a roller coaster scene for their video, *You're Invited to Mary-Kate & Ashley's Birthday Party*. To get the scene, the whole group had to ride the roller coaster eight times in a row! "We all got so dizzy we could hardly stand," Ashley remembers.

Now that they're older, Mary-Kate and Ashley don't ride roller coasters much. They're too busy riding in their cars! Each received a brand-new car for her sixteenth birthday.

Mary-Kate and Ashley: Our Story

"It's great to have more freedom. Sometimes we'll meet our friends at the beach or at the movies. Other times we just hang out at their houses," Mary-Kate says. "And when we're not driving someplace, there's always something fun to do at home – especially swimming. We have a pool in the back yard."

Ashley and Mary-Kate don't share a room. They have separate rooms at both their mom's and their dad's places. At their dad's, the rooms are down the hall from each other. They love the shabby-chic style of design and their rooms are decorated with pretty fabric patterns and tons of fluffy pillows.

Both girls have lots of pictures on the walls – pictures of friends, cast photos from movies they've worked on, and places they've visited all over the world. They also display photos of their parents and brothers and sisters.

Mary-Kate and Ashley each have their own stereo and TV in their bedrooms. When asked about their favourite TV shows, they answer at the exact same time: "We like *Will and Grace* and *Friends!*" They might add "late-night infomercials" to that list, too – both girls admit to falling asleep with the TV on!

When Mary-Kate and Ashley became teens, they

got their own computers. They were so excited, they took a typing course in school so they could type really fast on the keyboard. Both are hooked on the Internet, and they research subjects on the World Wide Web for school. And, of course, their friends across the country and around the world are just a click away through e-mail. Mary-Kate, especially, likes to keep in touch with all the friends she makes when they film a movie far from home.

The sisters – and their parents – take school very seriously. Their parents make sure that Mary-Kate and Ashley are getting the best education possible. Even when Mary-Kate and Ashley are working on a TV show or a movie, they don't miss a day of class. The classroom just has to go where they go!

"A lot of people probably think that going on location must be cool because then we get to miss school," says Ashley. "Wrong!"

"The law says we have to spend at least three hours each day in school and do a ton of homework while we're working," Mary-Kate explains. "Besides, when we're done shooting and go back home, we don't want to be behind the rest of our class."

Mary-Kate and Ashley keep up with their class-mates by having studio teachers right there on the set. The studio teachers give all the same homework and tests that their regular teachers give. Usually they have one teacher for language arts, French and social studies and one for maths and science.

The girls do well in all their school subjects. In fact, they like to compete with each other for the highest grades. "Ashley makes me work harder," Mary-Kate says. "If I don't do as well as Ashley on a test, I'll go over the subject again."

"The same goes for me," Ashley adds.

Ashley's favourite subject is maths. Mary-Kate enjoys English and creative writing. Sometimes Mary-Kate will write short stories on her own. And sometimes they both keep journals when they visit new places.

Ashley and Mary-Kate say their studio teachers can be tough when necessary to make sure all their homework gets done. "Sometimes they'll crack the whip to make sure we finish on time," Mary-Kate admits. "But actually, *we* want to get it done and over with just as much as they do!"

When the sisters are doing a TV show, the studio classroom looks just like a regular classroom – with desks, computers, and maps on the walls. But when Mary-Kate and Ashley are travelling to make a movie, they use any room that is available. "We've had classrooms in trailers, in lobbies – once even in a large cupboard!" Ashley remembers.

At the time this book was printed, Mary-Kate and Ashley were hard at work studying for finals and for their college entrance exams. "It's tough work," Mary-Kate says, "but we know we have to do it if we want to get into a good college."

But it's not all about work for Mary-Kate and Ashley. They try to have as much fun as possible while they're on the set. That's not always easy, though. Sometimes people are a little nervous being around them at first. But it doesn't take long for people to realise that Mary-Kate and Ashley don't *act* famous.

"I met Mary-Kate and Ashley on the set of *Holiday in the Sun*," recalls Billy Brown, an actor and friend who has appeared in three of their movies and on the television show *So Little Time*. "It was my first big break and I was excited to meet them. I was surprised at how shy they were at first. But then we got to talking, and they're really nice and a lot of fun. I have a blast every time I work with them."

They do their best to make everyone feel really comfortable. And Mary-Kate and Ashley are the first to reach out and help others in need. "They're genuinely good, sweet, compassionate girls," their studio teacher says.

So how can Mary-Kate and Ashley be stars *and* be so much like you and your friends? They say they have their mom and dad to thank.

"The most important thing our parents have taught us is to respect other people," Mary-Kate says. "After all, we're only two of six kids in our family. There's no time for special treatment."

"Yeah," Ashley agrees. "We have to clean our rooms just like everybody else."

Chapter 2

The Twin Thing

In a lot of ways Mary-Kate and Ashley are like you and your friends. And if you have a twin, then they *really* are like you!

"People ask us all the time if it's fun to be a twin," Mary-Kate says, "and we always tell them the same thing. Yes!"

"We always have each other to talk with," Ashley explains. "We share all our big secrets."

Sisters are often very close. But twin sisters are built-in best friends! Like most twins, Mary-Kate and Ashley share a special bond. Each of them often seems to know what the other is thinking – without saying a word.

"Ashley can tell things about me, like if something is bothering me – or if I think a guy is cute!" Mary-Kate says.

"We can tell what the other is feeling, but we can't read each other's minds or anything," Ashley adds. "It's more like understanding body language."

The girls have a great time together. Mary-Kate is known to be more of a prankster, but both girls have a great sense of humour. In fact, Ashley usually jumps right in on Mary-Kate's practical jokes. But it's all in the name of fun. When they're on a set, Mary-Kate and Ashley's favourite prank is to clip a clothes peg on the back of a co-worker's shirt. Then they'll wait – and giggle – to see how long it takes before he or she notices! "It's a long-running joke," Ashley explains. "We've been doing it since we were kids. So we keep doing it just to crack each other up."

Being a twin isn't just fun. There are other bene-fits, too. Think about how practical it would be to have someone who looks like you – especially if you both had the same taste in clothes.

When Mary-Kate and Ashley were younger they didn't always have to try on their clothes before buying them. Who needs a mirror when you can see how an outfit looks on your twin, right?

Unfortunately that trick doesn't work for Ashley

and Mary-Kate any more. They still have similar taste in clothes, but Mary-Kate leans towards more funky outfits and lots of accessories, where Ashley likes classic and tailored items – and shoes, shoes, shoes!

Another example of how having a twin can come in handy was when the girls filmed their first TV movie *To Grandmother's House We Go*. Just a week before filming began, Mary-Kate scratched her eye while playing. It was red for weeks! They filmed around it as much as possible, but when it came to an important dinner scene between the two girls, Ashley got dressed like Mary-Kate and played both parts!

Of course, everyone always expects twins to trade places with each other. You've seen it on TV shows, where twins switch places to take a test in school. Or to go out on a date. Or to fool a friend. In one episode of Mary-Kate and Ashley's TV series, *TWO of a kind*, the girls switched places to fool their dad. They did it again in their TV movie *Switching Goals* and in their feature film, *It Takes Two*. But Mary-Kate and Ashley swear they've never done that in real life.

"We haven't tried it," Ashley tells us. "Our friends and family can tell us apart. So we never bothered."

Mary-Kate and Ashley were born on June 13, under the sign of Gemini. It makes sense – Gemini is the sign of twins! Geminis often have great communication skills, just like Mary-Kate and Ashley. They are fun-loving, outgoing, and quick-minded. Geminis can also adapt easily to new situations. And best of all, just like Mary-Kate and Ashley, Geminis love people – especially their friends!

Or maybe they just don't remember. "They did try some switcheroos around age five," their mom says. "But ultimately they can't fool me or their dad."

Well, most of the time, anyway. Once, when the twins were shooting a video, their dad called out, "Ashley, come here. I want to ask you something." But he was really talking to Mary-Kate! The whole film crew laughed. Their dad's mistake probably made the crew feel better about all the times *they'd* got Mary-Kate and Ashley mixed up.

Still, it isn't always easy to guess who's who. Everyone seems to come up with a different way to tell Mary-Kate and Ashley apart.

"Bob Saget, our TV dad on *Full House*, used to mix us up all the time when we were little," recalls Mary-Kate.

"We'd put our hands on our hips and give him our best 'Don't-you-know-me-by-now?' look," Ashley adds, laughing. "After we got a little older and he got to know our personalities, he was finally able to tell us apart."

Even their hairstylist sometimes got them confused. "He'd forget whose hair he was working on and ask, 'Which one are you again?'" Mary-Kate remembers.

But Mary-Kate and Ashley don't get mad when people mistake them for each other. They're used to it. They just smile and say, "My name is Ashley (or Mary-Kate), not Mary-Kate (or Ashley)!"

Even though the girls look so much alike, they are not identical twins. Mary-Kate and Ashley are fraternal twins. Fraternal twins sometimes look similar to each other, but they are not exactly the same.

There *are* ways to tell Mary-Kate and Ashley apart. When Mary-Kate and Ashley were infants, their parents used their freckles to figure out who was who. Now, at sixteen, Ashley is slightly taller. Mary-Kate's face is a bit rounder. Ashley is right-handed, while Mary-Kate is left-handed.

"I think we looked more alike when we were younger, but not now," Ashley says.

DID YOU KNOW?

- Spring is the time of the year that most twins are born (just like Mary-Kate and Ashley, who were born in June).
- More than half of all twins are male.
- More twins are left-handed, like Mary-Kate, than are people who are not twins.
- Fraternal twins, like Mary-Kate and Ashley, are more likely to run in the family than are identical twins.
- Female fraternal twins and their sisters are more likely to give birth to twins.

"I'm the cute one," jokes Mary-Kate. "Just kidding. Seriously, I don't think we look anything alike."

For work, the girls have often had to look as similar as possible – especially during their time on *Full House*, when they played the same part. But Ashley and Mary-Kate enjoy trying out different looks.

A couple of years ago, the sisters decided to change their hairstyle. Mary-Kate cut her hair shorter. It was cute and it looked great on her. For a while, she clearly had her own look.

There was just one problem: Ashley loved her sister's short hair – and she wanted her own hair cut the same way. Before they knew it, the girls looked alike again. Over the past few years they've tried many styles – short, long, straight, curly. Hey, they're teens and they like to experiment!

Currently the makeup look of choice for both girls is a fresh face with a hint of lip gloss for everyday. But they'll break out the makeup brushes if they have a special event to attend.

And since they have similar fashion sense, sometimes they buy the same outfits or accessories for an event, but each girl picks a different colour so they never end up dressing alike.

But what happens when they both want to wear the exact same thing on the same day?

"When Mary-Kate and Ashley want to wear the same outfit, it gets a little crazy," their dad says with a laugh. He remembers when the girls were getting dressed for a concert. They both wanted to wear the same brown jacket with their black trousers. This time, Mary-Kate won – and she got to wear it. (Ashley wore a blue jacket.) The next time, Ashley got to pick first. When they were younger, the girls were also known to argue over who had the cooler, more grown-up shoes.

So, how do Mary-Kate and Ashley work out their occasional differences? "We talk it over, and then we usually decide to take turns," Ashley explains. "Mary-Kate will wear something one time and I'll wear it the next time."

In fact, the girls don't compete with each other at all. Well, except for grades. "But it's good-natured, and it pushes us to do better, " Mary-Kate says.

Mary-Kate and Ashley look out for each other and give each other advice. And when they're acting, they always help each other out. For instance, during the filming of their movie *Passport to Paris*, Mary-Kate had to give a speech about Notre Dame Cathedral. It included lots of hard-to-remember words like "flying buttresses" (an architectural term) – and Mary-Kate kept tripping up on the words! Ashley gently touched her shoulder and said, "Don't worry, you'll get it." Later, when Ashley had to say a long speech in French, Mary-Kate was able to encourage *her*.

The girls make a terrific team because they are so supportive of each other. Sure, they can get on each other's nerves. All sisters do. They have sibling squabbles just like in any family. But in the end, Ashley and Mary-Kate are best friends.

"Having a twin keeps us grounded," Ashley says. "We encourage each other all the time, but we also know when to say, 'hey, get over yourself.'"

The Twin Thing

Recently a TV interviewer asked Ashley and Mary-Kate if they wanted to go to different colleges. Mary-Kate said, "I don't think so. Going to college is such an important time in your life. You know, a new place, new people, new experiences. I don't think I could be without my sister, too."

"Me neither," Ashley agrees. "She's always been there for me," says Ashley about her sister. "She's everything to me."

Chapter 3

The *Full House* Years

How did Mary-Kate and Ashley get started in show business?

It all began when they were just seven months old. Their mom took them to a modelling agency. Mary-Kate and Ashley were beautiful babies. And the fact that they were twins was a bonus. When kids are working on a movie or a television series, the law says they can work only for a few hours each day. Hiring twins means you are able to split the work between them.

The modelling agency quickly signed up both girls and lined up auditions. But Jarnie didn't expect that they would actually get work. "I just thought it might be fun," she admits. "It was a way to get out of the house and do something a little out of the ordinary."

Then Jarnie took the girls to a TV audition with executive producer Bob Boyett. Mr. Boyett was looking for young twins to play baby Michelle on a new ABC comedy. The show was called *Full House*.

By the time Mary-Kate and Ashley had their audition, there was already another set of twins in place to play the part of baby Michelle. But Mr. Boyett changed his mind when he met the Olsens. "I just thought they were so unique," he says. "They had these big expressive eyes. They were friendly, they listened when you spoke to them, and they would really respond to you!"

Plus, the girls looked a lot like the two big sisters on the TV show. Candace Cameron had been hired to play D.J., and Jodie Sweetin would play middle sister Stephanie.

Mary-Kate and Ashley were perfect for *Full House!* The fact that they were fraternal – not identical – twins could have been a problem, though. As babies, the girls looked almost exactly alike, so they could both be Michelle. But what would happen as the girls grew up? Would they still look alike?

Maybe you've seen the classic TV show *Bewitched* on Nickelodeon. On that show, twins were hired to play the role of baby Tabitha. But when they got older, their looks changed enough that you could tell them apart! Eventually one twin was chosen to continue playing the part.

But that didn't happen to Ashley and Mary-Kate!

Full House was a comedy about a different kind of family: three grown men raising three little girls. Danny Tanner, played by actor Bob Saget, was the dad. Danny had just lost his wife in a car accident and was left to raise his three daughters, D.J., Stephanie and Michelle, by himself. But he needed help. So his best friend, Joey (played by comic Dave Coulier), and brother-in-law Jesse (actor John Stamos), moved in to help out.

The three men didn't have very much in common. Danny was a television announcer, Joey was a stand-up comic and part-time inventor, and Jesse wanted to be a rock-and-roll singer. There was always something crazy going on in that household!

By the time the show began in September 1987, Ashley and Mary-Kate were already a year old. Most of their first scenes involved Michelle just being a baby. Ashley and Mary-Kate didn't have to do much. Uncle Joey would make a mess changing Michelle's nappy. Uncle Jesse would sing her a lullaby. Michelle would try to take a few steps.

The *Full House* Years

As the producers worked more and more with Mary-Kate and Ashley, they saw what special talents each of them could bring to the show. Although they looked alike, each twin had a distinct personality. "The girls could play so many different emotions because Ashley and Mary-Kate were so different," says their mom.

Once the producers realised that, it was easy to decide which twin would play which scene. In the early years, baby Ashley handled the sensitive scenes. Mary-Kate got the scenes where Michelle needed to be tough and sassy. As the girls' personalities developed, so did their roles. "Ashley became more serious, so she was given the serious lines," says their mom. "When they needed someone to be more active or emotional, they let Mary-Kate do it."

As infants, the girls sometimes needed acting

DID YOU KNOW?
- The Tanner address is 1882 Gerard Street.
- All of the Tanner kids attended Frasier Street Elementary School.
- Michelle's birthday is in November.
- Jesse's last name was Cochran, but in the fourth season he changed it to his family's Greek name, Katsopolis.

help. A cookie was often held in front of them so they would smile or giggle for the camera. And the girls' funny reactions helped make the show popular. When Mary-Kate and Ashley could finally speak, they learned their lines by mimicking their acting coach. The girls really impressed their coach because they were always willing to try something new. And they never said no to her. When they were old enough to read, they read and memorised their lines just like the other actors.

Baby Michelle was a hit! People were saying there was something special about *Full House*. Never before had a show dared to give a baby such a big part, week after week. But this time Mary-Kate and Ashley made it possible.

More and more people tuned in to see the show – and the amazing Michelle Tanner. And after a couple of seasons *Full House* became one of the top ten shows on television!

"I think it was the first time anyone really had a chance to watch a baby grow up on television," says the girls' mom. "They captured the audience's hearts."

Full House's Uncle Joey, actor Dave Coulier, agrees: "I think Mary-Kate and Ashley quickly grabbed a large piece of the audience by being really cute and by having their little catch phrases like 'You got it, dude,' and 'No way, José.'"

Viewers were thrilled that Michelle was played by twins. The show hyped the fact by having Ashley and Mary-Kate appear opposite each other. Two Michelles would sometimes appear together in a dream. Once, Michelle even met her look-alike cousin from Greece.

The girls were unaware of all the excitement around them. They never realised how popular they were. Every day Mary-Kate and Ashley just looked forward to going to the Warner Bros. Studios lot in Burbank, California, to see their "family" of co-workers. "The lot and the set were like a second home to us," says Mary-Kate.

The girls had fun playing with their young co-stars and with the golden retriever who played Comet. Jodie Sweetin and some of the kid guest stars would often visit Mary-Kate and Ashley in their dressing room. The girls got to decorate the room the way they wanted. It was full of games and art supplies. They often watched videos of classic musicals such as *Oklahoma!*, *Guys and Dolls*, *My Fair Lady*, and *West Side Story*.

It's no wonder that Ashley and Mary-Kate went on to star in so many musical videos of their own.

Going to the studio was a comfortable experience for them. "We grew up around all the people on *Full House*," says Mary-Kate. "That's what made it so much fun for us to go to work every day. We didn't do it because we had to. We did it because we loved it." The girls even complained about not working on Saturdays.

As Mary-Kate and Ashley got older, the show began featuring episodes that mirrored what was

---

DID YOU KNOW?
- The Tanners' phone number is 555-2424.
- D.J.'s private phone number is 555-8722.
- Michelle's middle name is Elizabeth.
- Tahj Mowry, who played Michelle's friend, Teddy, is the younger brother of twins Tia and Tamera Mowry from *Sister Sister*.

---

really happening in their lives: starting kindergarten. Learning to read. Riding a bicycle for the first time. Playing soccer. Dancing. Even Mary-Kate's love of horses was written into the story when Michelle took up riding.

As the series continued, Mary-Kate and Ashley's talent shone even brighter. "We were delighted," says their producer. "As they grew up they were learning from the very talented comedians on the show. And they began acting on their own very early. Mary-Kate and Ashley weren't having lines fed to them. They were studying acting and taking classes and becoming very good actresses."

Mary-Kate and Ashley don't have much time these days to watch television. But every once in a while they'll catch an old rerun of *Full House* on the cable station *Nick at Nite*. Like lots of actors, Ashley and Mary-Kate don't really enjoy watching themselves on screen. They are their own toughest critics. "Sometimes we look at what we did back then and think we could have done it better," Mary-Kate admits. *Full House* fans may not agree.

After eight years the show finally came to an end in 1995. But eight years is a great success in television. In fact, *Full House* is one of ABC's longest-running comedies ever!

There's an extra bonus for Mary-Kate and Ashley and their family. They have an incredible video collection of the sisters growing up, and they didn't even have to break out their own video camera!

Mary-Kate and Ashley still miss working on *Full House*. They especially miss their TV family. "It's sad not being with the 'other family' we grew up with," says Mary-Kate. So Ashley and Mary-Kate do try to stay in touch with the *Full House* bunch. They all get together for special events. Ashley and Mary-Kate attended baby showers for their co-stars Candace Cameron Bure (D.J.) and Lori Loughlin (Rebecca). And they were also at the wedding of John Stamos (Uncle Jesse), who married supermodel Rebecca Romijn. Seeing their friends is always fun, but the girls admit it sometimes makes them even more "homesick" for their *Full House* days.

After the super-successful show ended, some people thought Mary-Kate and Ashley's acting careers were over. But they were wrong! Amazing new opportunities were in store for Mary-Kate and Ashley. Their exciting careers were just beginning!

Chapter 4

From TV to Video – and Lots In Between

Starring in over twenty-five videos and nine movies, Mary-Kate and Ashley have the same, if not more, experience than many of the adults in the entertainment industry. But just how did two little girls turn into two of the most powerful people in Hollywood?

Because of their huge popularity on *Full House*, fans couldn't get enough of Mary-Kate and Ashley. Their fans wanted to see *both* of the girls acting at the same time.

Mary-Kate and Ashley each loved the idea – and that's how their first television movie was born! It was called *To Grandmother's House We Go*, and each girl had a starring role. The girls made the movie during their summer break in 1992. When it aired on TV a few months later, it was one of the most-watched movies of the season.

The experience of making their first movie is something the sisters will always treasure – especially Mary-Kate. You know how people say actors are always falling in love with their co-stars on the set. Well, six-year-old Mary-Kate was no different – except, of course, that the co-star she fell in love with was a pony!

"She was always talking about this miniature pony named Four-by-Four," Ashley remembers with a smile. "And whenever Mary-Kate was missing, we knew exactly where to find her: in the stable grooming *her* horse."

For months afterwards, when asked if she liked any boys in her school, Mary-Kate would merely grin and say, "I have a crush on Four-by-Four." One day Mary-Kate's dad even found her packing to go and visit the horse. Unfortunately, the pony lived in Vancouver, Canada – far away from the girls' home in Los Angeles.

"I had a plan," Mary-Kate says. "I was going to walk to the airport and take a plane. Don't ask me how I was going to buy a ticket. Dad found me before I figured out that part."

From TV to Video – and Lots In Between

To Grandmother's House We Go was a turning point for Ashley and Mary-Kate. The movie showed everyone that the girls were an important Hollywood team. They could play individual roles – not just share the role of the TV character Michelle Tanner. Together they would go on to make films, home videos, television specials, music albums, and even a series of books based on their video characters, the Trenchcoat Twins. And they were still just kids!

Mary-Kate and Ashley's first album, *Brother for Sale*, was a hit, too. "When we were rehearsing it, Trent would say, 'I hate that song!'" recalls Ashley.

"So I'd walk around the house saying 'My favourite song is "Brother for Sale",' especially when Trent was around," Mary-Kate remembers with a grin.

"But we love our brother," Ashley is quick to point out.

In 1993, the girls released their first music video, called simply *Our First Video*. It featured a collection of songs from Mary-Kate and Ashley's first two albums, *Brother for Sale* and *I Am the Cute One*. The sisters worked with a dance teacher to learn dance steps for the songs. But a lot of what ended up in the final video was the girls just having a blast, jumping around and bouncing on the bed!

Our First Video was a big success for Ashley and

Mary-Kate. To celebrate, they took eight of their friends to a restaurant for all the hamburgers and milkshakes they could eat – and they went in a limo.

"I remember that day," Mary-Kate says. "It was such a big deal to ride in a limousine. We were all so excited."

"I don't know," Ashley admits. "I still feel kind of special when I get to ride in a limo."

Even though Mary-Kate and Ashley made quite a splash with their music, they still wanted to act. Their second TV movie for ABC was a spooky Hallowe'en film called *Double, Double, Toil and Trouble*.

"We had a great time making that movie," Ashley recalls, "because of all the crazy costumes we wore. Mary-Kate and I have always loved spooky stories."

1994 was a big year for Mary-Kate and Ashley. The two made an appearance in the film *The Little Rascals*. The girls show up in a slumber party scene. Rent it and see if you can spot them!

Later Mary-Kate and Ashley made the TV movie *How the West Was Fun*. "I remember being so psyched about that project because I'd get to ride a horse again."

But the big news from Mary-Kate and Ashley that year was the grand opening of the Olsen and

From TV to Video – and Lots In Between

Olsen Mystery Agency. They got to play detectives in *The Adventures of Mary-Kate & Ashley*, a series of mystery videos. Nicknamed the "Trenchcoat Twins," the two adopted the motto "Will Solve Any Crime by Dinner Time." They were helped by their basset hound sidekick, Clue. The girls investigated mysteries in lots of exciting locations. The videos were shot in a spooky amusement park, aboard a U.S. Navy destroyer, at Sea World of Florida, at a volcano in Hawaii, and at many other amazing places. "We had a blast making those videos," Ashley says. "It was like playing all the time."

Mary-Kate and Ashley fans loved *The Adventures of Mary-Kate & Ashley* videos so much that a series of books based on the videos soon followed. The books were so popular that a new series of books was created called *The New Adventures of Mary-Kate & Ashley*. These books aren't based on the videos. They are all-new, original mysteries for the Trenchcoat Twins to solve.

Ashley and Mary-Kate are involved in the writing of each book. "We meet with the editors and tell them things we like to do," says Mary-Kate. "I like to horseback ride, so there is a horseback riding adventure. We both like to surf, so there's a surfing book. And Ashley likes ballet, so we did a ballet story." Today Mary-Kate and Ashley have a total of *six* different book series in bookstores!

Mary-Kate and Ashley's videos are created the same way the books are created. The girls' real lives are turned into fun, musical stories. That's how their second series of videos, *You're Invited to Mary-Kate & Ashley's,* came about. The girls loved to throw parties for their friends. By making these videos, they could share the fun with their fans.

The girls began with one of their favourite parties, *Sleepover Party*, and then the parties started getting bigger. They learned how to surf for their *Hawaiian Beach Party* and how to ski for their *Christmas Party.*

In 1995, something really big happened to Ashley and Mary-Kate. They got to star in their very first feature film! Now you could see them in your neighbourhood movie theatre *and* on TV! The movie was called *It Takes Two*, and in it the girls played identical "strangers," one rich and one poor. When they discover each other, they come up with a scheme to make their guardians fall in love. The movie was a huge favourite and is in video stores.

For Mary-Kate and Ashley, one of the best things about making videos and movies is that they get to travel to really exciting places. One of their family's favourite vacation spots is Hawaii. So guess what?

In 1996, the entire family went on a Hawaiian surf-and-sun vacation while Mary-Kate and Ashley made some videos there!

"We made four videos that vacation," Ashley recalls. *"You're Invited to Mary-Kate & Ashley's Hawaiian Beach Party. The Case Of The Hotel Who-Done-It. The Case Of The Volcano Mystery* and *The Case Of The U.S. Navy Adventure."*

"My favourite was *Hotel Who-Done-It*," Mary-Kate remembers. "I was really into chocolate back then, and our hotel refrigerator was stocked full. We had to eat it all for the video. In real life, anything you eat gets added to your hotel bill, but this time it was free! I was in total heaven."

"I'll never forget the video we did after Hawaii," Ashley says. "It was called *The Case Of The U.S. Space Camp Mission*, and we had to wear fake teeth!"

This video was shot at a real U.S. Space Camp in Huntsville, Alabama. At the time of the shoot, nine-year-olds Mary-Kate and Ashley were both missing a few of their teeth. So the gaps wouldn't show on video, the girls each used fake front teeth called "flippers." But when they left home for U.S. Space Camp, they left their "teeth" on their bathroom counter.

"We wound up running around Huntsville looking for a dentist to make our emergency flippers!"

Mary-Kate remembers. "Luckily, we found someone to help us get our teeth in place just in time!"

Still, false teeth or not, to this day Mary-Kate and
Ashley say that filming *The Case Of The U.S. Space
Camp Mission* was one of the most thrilling experiences in their careers. When they made the video,
they actually attended the space camp in Huntsville.
"Trent, Dad, Ashley and I went to a weekend
Parent-Child session," says Mary-Kate. "We were
each given different assignments to plan and carry
out on a pretend space shuttle mission. We also got
to work at mission control, build and launch model
rockets 400 feet high, and operate shuttle simulators. Trent loves video games, so he really went
wild!"

The highlight of Mary-Kate and Ashley's U.S.
Space Camp experience was having dinner with a
famous astronaut, Alan Bean. Alan Bean was the
fourth astronaut to walk on the moon during the
Apollo XII mission in 1970. (Apollo XII was the second spaceship to land on the moon.) "We felt so
honoured to have dinner with one of only twelve
people on Earth who have ever touched the moon,"
says Ashley.

"I'll never forget that evening," Mary-Kate recalls.
"Even though we were just young kids, he answered

all our questions and made us understand what it was like to travel in space."

For the video, the girls suited up as astronauts. Then they rode in space simulators, where they could experience how it would really feel to walk on the moon. "It was a strange sensation," says Mary-Kate. "Half walking. Half floating."

Even though she loved working in Hawaii and at Space Camp, Ashley's favourite video is no surprise: *Ballet Party*, with the New York City Ballet! Finally, she had a chance to show off her dancing talent. "I got to live out one of my big dreams," says Ashley. "We had to practise with a choreographer for days before the actual shoot. Because I had taken dance lessons for so long, I had a pretty good idea of what the steps were. But you should have seen Mary-Kate!"

Mary-Kate admits she was a bit nervous about getting up on stage – especially since the other girls in the video were students at a famous performing arts school called the Juilliard School of Dance. But Mary-Kate held her own.

"Whether you're a dancer or an athlete, you have to have a lot of strength and coordination," Ashley says. "Well, Mary-Kate had both. She worked really hard at all those pliés and jetés, and she was great. I think she surprised everyone, especially herself."

Mary-Kate and Ashley: Our Story

Mary-Kate had the upper hand for their next video. *Camp Out Party* was right in Mary-Kate's neck of the woods! Sleeping in a tent. Hiking in fresh air. Fishing and roasting marshmallows. "Not a few of Ashley's favourite things," Mary-Kate teases, "but we managed to get her there anyhow."

Whether it was dancing on their toes, going on a Space Mission, or skiing in the Rockies, Mary-Kate and Ashley were willing to give anything a try. Their fans around the world couldn't wait to see what they tried next.

Mary-Kate and Ashley would not disappoint them. In 1998, the sisters released their first *ninety-minute* direct-to-video movie called *Billboard Dad*. Again, Mary-Kate and Ashley got to do things they enjoy in real life. Mary-Kate played Tess, a surfer, and Ashley played Emily, a high diver. In the story, the girls teamed up to find a new love for their single dad – by placing an ad on a billboard!

Billboard Dad was the first of many full-length direct-to-video movies that Mary-Kate and Ashley would star in – movies that their fans would enjoy again and again.

Chapter 5

Shining Stars

Lights! Camera! Action!

Billboard Dad was great fun to make, and Ashley and Mary-Kate discovered that the change from a thirty-minute video to a ninety-minute video was triple the fun.

But it was hard work, too. It takes much more time to learn all the dialogue and shoot all the scenes and much more planning to get all the details – sets, lighting, wardrobe, and so on – just right! And when you're the exectuive producers of a film as well as the stars – as Mary-Kate and Ashley are – it's a lot of responsiblilty. But Mary-Kate and Ashley welcomed the challenge, and they always found a way to mix hard work with fun!

Mary-Kate and Ashley: Our Story

"In *Passport to Paris* I played Melanie and Ashley played Allison," Mary-Kate explains. "We're sent to stay with our grandfather in Paris, France during spring break." Of course, it wouldn't be any fun if the girls didn't get into mischief while seeing the sights of the city . . . or while riding around Paris on motor scooters with cute boys!

Well, that part was fun, but another part of the movie proved to be a bit more challenging.

Ashley was supposed to speak some French in the movie. So when the girls got to Paris, they both decided to speak the language whenever they could. Their French tutor travelled with them and they experimented on their own. They did their best to order in French while dining out. Once they were even daring enough to try *escargots* – snails! Snails are a delicacy in France. Ashley thought they were *"très bon,"* while Mary-Kate made it clear in English that she didn't care for the dish: "Yuck!"

But what really took guts for Mary-Kate and Ashley came in the boy department. *Passport to Paris* was their first romantic comedy. At thirteen they were each going to have their first screen kiss – and they would have to pull it off with a crew of fifty people standing around watching! And on the very first day they met the boys! Talk about pressure! The girls admit they were a little shy about having their first kisses in front of an audience. But they got plenty of chances to get used to it: they had to do it several times to get it just right for the camera!

"If you want to make movies," Mary-Kate says, "you can't be afraid of being embarrassed. You have to do your job in front of a group of people. So you have to be ready to put yourself out there."

Big crowds are nothing new when you're on the set of a Mary-Kate and Ashley movie. In *Holiday in the Sun*, the girls play Madison and Alex, who stumble across a smuggling ring in the Bahamas. It was filmed at the beautiful Atlantis resort on Paradise Island. Since the movie was shot in the summer, there were lots of families staying at the hotel, and that meant crowds of Mary-Kate and Ashley fans everywhere. Ashley and Mary-Kate were recognised wherever they went.

"Sometimes we were late to the set," Ashley recalls, "because we kept stopping to say hello and to sign autographs."

"I remember once when the producer picked me up from my room so that I wouldn't stop to talk to our fans," Mary-Kate says. "He suggested I wear a big hat and sunglasses so that I wouldn't be recognised, but I didn't think it would work."

And it didn't. The fans recognised Mary-Kate at once. The minute she and the producer entered the lobby, a bunch of girls came over and screamed out "Hi, Mary-Kate!" This was especially funny since several of the crew members on the set still couldn't tell Mary-Kate and Ashley apart.

One time that Mary-Kate and Ashley were *not* recognised was when they were filming *When In Rome.* In this movie, Mary-Kate and Ashley played Charli and Leila, two girls who become interns in the fashion department of a big Italian company.

"My character, Charli, had a crush on an Italian boy named Paolo," Mary-Kate says. "Paolo was played by Michaelangelo Tomasso, a famous actor in Italy. One day, when we were shooting a romantic scene in Rome, a group of Italian girls asked if they could take a picture with Michaelangelo – and they asked me to step away so I wouldn't be in the picture!"

"Sometimes when we're shooting on location we need to film a scene without any people in the background. This happened a few times during our shoot for *Winning London.* We got to go into Westminster Abbey before it opened," Ashley says. "It was an amazing feeling being in such a historic church." Westminster Abbey is over 900 years old, and most of England's kings and queens were crowned there. It is also the burial place for many important people in England's history, such as the famous author, Charles Dickens, poet, Robert Browning, and

DID YOU KNOW?
In *Winning London*, the boy who plays the English character, James, isn't English?
He's Australian!

scientists Sir Isaac Newton and Charles Darwin.

"It was also fun shooting at the Tower of London – until our time ran out!" Ashley tells us. "The security guards made us put away our cameras and stop filming. But to get just a little more, the director whipped out his home movie camera and shot as we were leaving. The home video footage is in the movie!"

"Being on a movie location is like being with a great big family," Mary-Kate says. "You get very close with the people you work with."

Winning London was about kids from all around the world, coming together to debate in the model UN. "It was a competition," Ashley says. "Our team was from the United States, and we were all supposed to be friends. And that's exactly what happened – in real life."

"It wasn't hard to imagine being good friends with these kids," Mary-Kate recalls. "There was a group of five of us. We had a blast!"

Mary-Kate and Ashley also have a special place in their hearts for their movie *Holiday in the Sun*. The movie was shot in the summer, so Ashley and Mary-Kate didn't have to worry about school. "We had so much fun playing on the beach and hanging out by the pool!" Mary-Kate remembers. "We all just clicked, you know. By the end of filming the group was really tight. I had a feeling that we'd stay in touch back home. I'm glad I was right."

"We met some amazing people on that shoot," Ashley agrees. "Lifelong friends."

"The cast and crew of a movie are all there to support one another," Ashley says. "So we don't have to be afraid to make mistakes."

"And there have been lots of them!" Mary-Kate laughs.

Passport to Paris was shot half in Paris and half in Los Angeles. All of the outside shots were done in Paris. Weeks later, the inside shots were filmed in a movie studio in Los Angeles. This worked fine for most of the movie, but if you look closely you can see a problem in one scene – the one where they are saying goodbye to everyone at the embassy.

Most of the scene was shot inside (in Los Angeles). But then everyone walks outside (shot in Paris). To make it work, the clothes had to be the same in both parts of the scene. But when they shipped the clothes from France to California, the dress that the character Bridget wore got lost. They had to try to make another dress. If you look very closely, you can see that the dresses are not exactly alike.

Getting There is about two girls who recently get their drivers' licences and take a road trip to the winter Olympics in Utah. There was a lot of skiing in that movie and one of the characters, Lindi, breaks her leg. "But that was never supposed to happen," Mary-Kate admits. "The actress who played Lindi had an accident while they were shooting and really did break her leg."

"That was a problem because now that she had a cast on her leg, she couldn't do some of the scenes that were in the script," Ashley says.

So what did they do?

They changed the story so that Lindi breaks her

leg and that way the actress could continue with the movie!

But a problem isn't always that easy to fix. Sometimes you encounter things you can't do anything about. "One time when we were shooting a movie, Mary-Kate got the giggles during a very serious scene," Ashley remembers. "She was laughing so hard that we had to stop shooting and take a break. After Mary-Kate calmed down we started shooting again. I turned to my sister and asked, 'Are you okay now?' and then *I* started laughing!"

"Soon the entire crew was laughing," adds Mary-Kate. "It took about twenty minutes to get everyone calmed down and quiet."

But Mary-Kate and Ashley admit that their toughest problem occurred in *The Challenge*. Why? Because nearly everyone on the set got sick from the water in Mexico! "They call it Montezuma's Revenge," Mary-Kate says. "It's kind of funny, now that I can look back on it. You know, since the video is called *The Challenge*."

But you never see any of the problems on film. That's the magic of the movies.

Problems or not, Mary-Kate and Ashley are always ready to jump in when the director yells "action" – and we mean ACTION!

In *Holiday In the Sun*, Mary-Kate and Ashley were the first ones to hop on jet skis, swoosh down a huge slide, or swim with the dolphins. In *Winning London* they learned how to play polo and how to fence!

Our Lips Are Sealed followed Mary-Kate and Ashley as they unsuccessfully tried to hide out from bad guys in Australia. Mary-Kate and Ashley marvelled at how beautiful the country was and loved shooting a movie "down under."

"It took fourteen hours to get there, but it was so worth it," Ashley says. "We got to do a lot of surfing in that movie," Ashley says. "We learned how to do it from a champion surfer!"

The stunts in *Our Lips Are Sealed* weren't always so easy. One time they had to work with a kangaroo.

"Vince the kangaroo was so cuddly and friendly, Ashley and I just wanted to take him home," remembers Mary-Kate.

Too bad they couldn't. Mary-Kate and Ashley shot only part of *Our Lips Are Sealed* in Australia. The other part was filmed in a Los Angeles movie studio. When Mary-Kate and Ashley returned home to finish shooting the rest of the movie they had to work with a different kangaroo – only this

Mary-Kate and Ashley's Surfing Lingo

Wipeout: when you are thrown off the board into the ocean.

Over the falls: a wipeout when the wave crashes over you and you are thrown up over it, like going over a waterfall.

Tubed: surfing inside the wave, under the curl.

Stoked: feeling excited about the waves!

Floater: when you board up to the lip of the wave and float down while you ride the board.

Off the lip: when you are on the very top of the wave, you go through the edge of the wave and it forces you down.

Got the fever: feeling like you have to go out and surf!

kangaroo wasn't nearly as friendly as Vince. In fact, he was kind of crabby!

"We were a little nervous doing our scenes around the new kangaroo, but we were very professional about it. We got through it as fast as we could, and then it was *see you later!*" Ashley says. The next time you watch *Our Lips Are Sealed*, see if you can tell the difference between Vince and the other kangaroo!

Another time during *Our Lips Are Sealed* Ashley

and Mary-Kate had to walk on top of the famous Sydney bridge that crosses Sydney harbour. It's very high and very scary. But the worst part was when a thunderstorm was breaking out in the distance while Mary-Kate and Ashley were up there. The girls had to get off that bridge fast or possibly be hit by lightning!

Mary-Kate and Ashley had to cross another bridge in one of their more recent movies, *The Challenge*. This bridge was hung over jagged rocks, and it was made of rope. It was the kind of bridge that sways from side to side when you cross it, and it can flip over! And Mary-Kate and Ashley's characters had to cross it in order to win a *Survivor*-type competition.

"The crew was nervous about us walking the bridge – even with the safety harnesses," Ashley recalls. "But Mary-Kate and I were up for it."

Another "challenge" involved balancing on a tall telephone pole, which was standing out in the ocean. "The top of the pole was about the size of a plate," Ashley remembers. "And I had to stand on it for almost an hour without falling into the water."

There are times when you *think* you're seeing something in a movie, but it's really a fake. For example, in a scene from *The Challenge*, Mary-Kate has to eat worms. And it really looks like she is!

Yes, Mary-Kate had to dip her hand into a gross plate of real worms. But when you see her eat one, it's only a brown Gummi Worm.

Mary-Kate throws a boomerang perfectly in *Our Lips Are Sealed*. It always comes right back to her. How did she manage to do this? More movie magic. Mary-Kate threw the boomerang, but then the film-makers used computer imaging to show the boomerang going just where it had to go.

In *Billboard Dad*, the girls paint a giant billboard on Sunset Boulevard in Los Angeles. It wouldn't be safe to do that for real – so☐ high up with traffic below. So the filmmakers made a small billboard on a sound stage, then they shot the scene with a plain green screen in the background. Later, through the magic of movies, they inserted Sunset Boulevard in the background.

In *Getting There*, Mary-Kate and Ashley had to drive a car, but they had only learners' permits. That meant they needed an adult in the car with them when they were driving, but the scenes they were shooting didn't call for an adult to be in the car. What did they do? That's right – more movie magic! Off camera, the car was towed. On camera, it looked as if Ashley and Mary-Kate were actually driving!

As Mary-Kate and Ashley get older, their movies reflect the changes in their lifestyles. That's why independence is such a strong theme in *Getting There*. In this movie, Mary-Kate and Ashley play girls who are about to take their first road trip – to the winter Olympics in Utah!

"*Getting There* was a little closer to home for us, and I don't mean because it was made in the United States," Mary-Kate says. "It reflects our real life in a way. At the time we made the movie, Ashley and I were just learning how to drive ourselves."

"Yeah," Ashley agrees. "We wanted to get in as much driving time as possible. We still do."

Mary-Kate and Ashley like to make movies that are fun for them to do – and just as fun for you to watch. Now that Ashley and Mary-Kate are older, they are much more involved in the "behind the scenes" action of their movies than when they were kids. "We love acting," Ashley points out, "but it's just as important to know what to look for from behind the camera as it is to know what your character is all about."

Now, as executive producers of their movies, Mary-Kate and Ashley not only pick the locations of their movies, they help the other producers and the writers come up with cool stories. "They'll give us a bunch of ideas and we'll tell them what we like and what we don't like," Ashley says. "And sometimes the writers will work from ideas that we come up with."

Mary-Kate and Ashley also play a big role in the writing of their scripts. "We want to make sure that our movies are entertaining," Mary-Kate says.

To do that, they give the writers their comments on scripts and the writers make changes. A script has to get the okay from Mary-Kate and Ashley before production on a movie can begin. In addition, Ashley and Mary-Kate are very involved in casting, and they work with the other producers to choose actors for their movies. They also decide which songs will be used for their movie soundtracks.

On top of all that, Mary-Kate and Ashley play a role behind the camera. Many times, after Ashley or Mary-Kate act in a scene, they will watch it on a monitor to make sure the scene is right. They'll make comments like "That was good!" or "I can do better. Let's try it again."

"It's great experience," Ashley admits, "since we'd like to try directing one day."

Until then, Ashley and Mary-Kate have their hands

full. In 2003, they released what is scheduled to be their final direct-to-video movie – *The Challenge*. But don't worry, Mary-Kate and Ashley won't be going away. They're moving on to the big screen!

The Challenge was filmed in Cabo San Lucas, Mexico. It's about a group of kids who are in a teen *Survivor*-type game, competing for college scholarships. Mary-Kate and Ashley play sisters who do *not* like each other. Their parents are divorced and one girl lives with their father in Washington while the other lives with their mother in Los Angeles.

Unfortunately they get put on the same team with a group of other kids, and Mary-Kate and Ashley are constantly fighting. They have to learn to work together or they'll blow it for everybody. Of course they learn to get along with each other by the end of the movie!

"It was a nice twist on the roles Mary-Kate and I usually play," Ashley says. "It was kind of fun to have a conflict between us."

"I really liked the *Survivor* aspect of the whole thing," Mary-Kate says. "And there's a cool surprise at the end," she adds. "But I don't want to give it away. You'll have to see it for yourself!"

What's next for Mary-Kate and Ashley? Well, they're working on making a major feature film for

Warner Bros. Studios!

"We were at a crossroads in our careers," Ashley says. "We had to decide if we wanted to keep doing the same thing or if we wanted to try something new."

"And we chose to go for it!" Mary-Kate adds.

Chapter 6

Television for Two

Mary-Kate and Ashley Olsen. Also known as *Michelle Tanner.* Also known as *Mary-Kate and Ashley Burke.* Also known as *Chloe and Riley Carlson.* Also known as *Special Agents Misty and Amber.* In four different series Ashley and Mary-Kate have always been favourites on television.

When *Full House* ended the sisters got busy with videos and movies. But in 1998, they were ready to return to TV. They starred in an ABC television series called *TWO of a kind.*

The show was about twin girls named Mary-Kate and Ashley! But instead of Olsen, their last name was Burke. "Our characters were opposites," Mary-Kate says. "The producers took some of our own personality differences and exaggerated them. I played a tomboy whose biggest interest was perfecting her curve ball. Ashley played a straight-A student who was starting to become interested in boys."

"I'm not as girlie in real life as I was on the show," Ashley says. And Mary-Kate agrees, "I'm not as sporty or tomboyish as my character. But the differences between the two characters made the show really funny."

The make-believe Burke family lived in Chicago with their single dad, a college professor. He was on the hunt for a baby-sitter to watch the girls after school and be a good role model.

Actor Christopher Seiber played Mary-Kate and Ashley's dad. The baby-sitter was played by Sally Wheeler. This was Chris and Sally's big television break. They would be working with seasoned pros Mary-Kate and Ashley, who had already been in show business for twelve years.

"On the first day I was terribly nervous," admits Sally. "I went up to the girls and said, 'Well, you guys, you know I've never actually done something like this. I'm so nervous.' And they said, 'Hey, don't worry. You can always do the scene again if you mess up. Come on, calm down.' Mary-Kate and Ashley were so generous and very helpful."

Sally found that she actually had a lot in common with Mary-Kate and Ashley. Like Mary-Kate, Sally had a passion for horses. And like both girls, Sally enjoyed Rollerblading. The three of them could often be found taking a break, skating around the Warner Bros. Studios lot.

After the first episode, or "pilot," was completed, Mary-Kate spoke up. She wanted her character to have a softer look. "She looked like a total tomboy," Mary-Kate said. "They kept bringing me out in a football or basketball uniform. I didn't really like that, so we changed it. My character was still a tomboy who liked to hang out with the guys. She loved to play football and basketball, but the way she dressed was a little different." Instead of sports jerseys, Mary-Kate got to wear jeans on the show. Ashley usually wore a dressier outfit. "That's definitely her style in real life," says Mary-Kate.

Unfortunately, *TWO of a kind* lasted only one season in its first run. "We were sad that it came to an end," says Ashley, "because for a season you kind of get attached to the people you're working with. But it wasn't like the end of *Full House*. *Full House* was something very special."

Two years later Ashley and Mary-Kate were back

with *So Little Time* on FOX Family channel (now ABC Family). But this television project was different from the others. This time Mary-Kate and Ashley were executive producers of their show. Not only did the sisters help come up with the idea, they were involved in lots of different ways, from scripts to casting to wardrobe. They became the first teens ever to produce and star in their own television series!

And it wasn't easy. *So Little Time* had a hectic schedule. Usually a weekly television show finishes filming one episode in about five days. Mary-Kate and Ashley shot more than one episode in *four* days.

Mary-Kate played Riley Carlson and Ashley starred as her sister, Chloe. "Our characters were more sophisticated then the Burke sisters," explains Mary-Kate. "Riley is into nature and saving the world. She's very spontaneous and no two days are alike for her. Chloe, on the other hand, is a creature of habit. She plays the mommy's girl, who is totally high-strung and a definite over-achiever."

If the character names sound familiar, then you probably remember them from *Winning London*. They liked the names so much they wanted to use them again. But just to keep you on your toes, the sisters decided to swap! In the movie, Mary-Kate played Chloe while Ashley played Riley.

The show's theme song also appeared in *Winning London*. "So Little Time" is performed by the British group Arcana and actually inspired the name of the television series!

On the show, on top of having normal teenage troubles, Riley and Chloe had to deal with the separation of their parents. Their mom, Macy, was a high-powered fashion designer living in a Malibu beach home. Their dad, Jake, was trying to "find himself" and moved into a tiny trailer nearby. Chloe and Riley lived with their mom but saw their dad all the time.

With both *TWO of a kind* and *So Little Time*, Ashley and Mary-Kate had to divide their day between work and school. They worked four days a week. Every morning they studied with their studio teachers for three hours. Their schoolwork at the studio matched the work their classmates were doing back at Mary-Kate and Ashley's regular school.

The sisters made twenty-six episodes of *So Little Time* but chose not to continue with any more. They made a deal with Warner Bros. to star in a feature film before they start college. To accomplish this,

Mary-Kate and Ashley had to take a break from TV in 2002.

Ironically, that same year, Mary-Kate received a nomination for a Daytime Emmy Award as "Outstanding Performer in a Children's Series." Even though she didn't win the gold statuette, it was still a great honour just to be considered.

Check out your cable stations for reruns of both *TWO of a kind* on CiTV, Fox Kids and the Disney Channel, and *So Little Time* on CBBC and CBBC digital.

And you can also see Mary-Kate and Ashley in animation on CiTV. In 2001 they executive produced and starred in the cartoon show *Mary-Kate and Ashley in ACTION!*

In this series Mary-Kate supplies the voice of Special Agent Misty, while Ashley plays Special Agent Amber, two hip teens who travel the world to fight crime and supervillains. While the Trenchcoat Twins had their basset hound sidekick Clue, Misty and Amber are aided by the fluffy white Quincy – a computerised canine who can talk!

"We spent a lot of time with the artists and writers to create this show," Mary-Kate says. "It took a real team effort to develop just the right look for Misty and Amber."

Here's a picture of us as babies.

Here we are at 7 years old with our favourite teddy bears.

Our first congratulatory business cake.

Here we are showing off our videos
and books at age 8.

Shooting our video _Christmas Party_ in Vail, Colorado gave us a chance to become ace skiers—sort of!

We love travelling the world to shoot new movies!
Here we are in Australia for Our Lips Are Sealed . . .

. . . and sightseeing in England
while making Winning London.

Feeding the pigeons in Venice, Italy.

Riding along the Venetian canals.

A family portrait, summer of 2001.
Top: mom, Jarnette; Trent; Lizzie. Bottom: Ashley; Mary-Kate.

A family portrait, summer of 2002. Top: Lizzie; Trent; stepmom, McKenzie; Mary-Kate; dad, Dave; Ashley. Bottom: Taylor; Jake.

We always have each other to lean on.
That's what sisters are for!

Television for Two

"And it was a new challenge, acting with only our voices," Mary-Kate adds. "We're really happy with how it turned out.

While Mary-Kate and Ashley are now working on a big-screen career, they'll always remember the fun they had on their television series.

"It's where we got our start," Ashley says. "It's where we grew up."

Chapter 7

The *mary-kateandashley* Brand

The music pulses as models prance down the runway in hot fashions for teens. The cameras flash as photographers take picture after picture of the newest *mary-kateandashley* brand clothes and accessories. And after the last model completes her walk, Mary-Kate and Ashley bound down the runway together. The cameras flash again, capturing them in their fabulous business suits.

Why are they wearing business suits? Because Mary-Kate and Ashley are not only fantastic actresses, they're savvy business women, too. Their apparel is the coolest thing in the stores.

But the *mary-kateandashley* brand fashion line didn't just happen overnight. At the age of ten, the sisters began working with executive designer, Judy Swartz. She would plan their outfits for their video and public appearances. The girls admit that they needed some help when it came to clothes back then. "I had my favourite shorts that I never took off," recalls Mary-Kate. "They were tight Spandex with fringe."

"She would wear those every day!" Ashley laughs. "And I only wore baggy clothes. We were pretty bad before Judy."

When Ashley and Mary-Kate did the TV series *TWO of a kind*, Judy was asked to put together the wardrobe for the show. Like other twelve-year-olds, Mary-Kate and Ashley wanted to look older and more sophisticated. To accomplish that, Judy bought them adult clothes and had them cut down to fit.

The unique look was a hit and fans wanted to know where they could get cool clothes like Ashley and Mary-Kate's. With Judy's design expertise, the sisters launched the *mary-kateandashley* brand of clothing at Wal-Mart stores across the country in early 2001.

The first season of clothes featured 1970s-inspired peasant blouses, tank tops, jeans, shoes, sleepwear, jeweller, and sunglasses. "Sometimes the fashion line is influenced by the clothes in our movies," Mary-Kate tells us.

"But mostly it's inspired by the fashions we wear and like," Ashley adds.

And what would a fashion line be without a grand runway show? Mary-Kate and Ashley showed off their new designs with a fun runway show and party in Hollywood. The fashion show was called Mary-Kate and Ashley Fashion Forward, and it was cybercast on AOL and aired on the Fox Family channel in the United States (now ABC Family).

The *mary-kateandashley* brand fashion line quickly became one of the fastest growing 'tween and teen clothing lines in America. Wal-Mart couldn't keep the items in stock! They sold out in a matter of weeks.

Mary-Kate and Ashley quickly got back into action to expand their clothing line. They play a big part in the design of each piece that is produced. "We're very involved in picking the clothing we want to see next season," says Ashley. "Judy will go to the fashion capitals of the world to look for new trends. Sometimes she'll find them at a fashion show. Other times she'll spot a guy or girl wearing an interesting outfit on the street."

"Then she'll come back to us with several trends

she thinks are going to be big," Mary-Kate says. "We'll tell her which ones we want to go with."

"Or sometimes we'll get inspired by something and come up with our own design idea and take it from there," Ashley adds.

"I work very closely with Mary-Kate and Ashley throughout the entire process," Judy points out. "I show them designs, fabrics and samples of finished products. They'll give me their opinions at every stage. Sometimes we'll need to make small changes. Other times we'll decide that a particular design isn't right for the line and start over."

"We're firm about what kinds of products we'll put our names on," Mary-Kate tells us. "It doesn't make sense to put out something we don't like."

"It seems to be working," Ashley says. "We have got some great feedback about *mary-kateandashley* brand fashions from the kids who wear them."

"Mary-Kate and Ashley have great fashion intuition," Judy adds. "So far they've been right every time."

Mary-Kate and Ashley love to wear lots of accessories – bracelets, rope or beaded chokers, ankle bracelets, and all sorts of jewellery.

"I love watches," Mary-Kate says. "I can't have enough of them!" "And don't forget shoes," Ashley adds. "Especially strappy sandals and flip flops!" In addition to a large collection of shoes, Ashley has a weakness for handbags.

Both girls have learned that the trick to looking great is feeling great. And that comes from having a good diet and getting plenty of exercise. Ashley and Mary-Kate both stay active with yoga. And they eat lots of fruits, salad and fish. The girls aren't really interested in sweets any more. And instead of soda, they'll usually reach for juice or water.

"I do have one big weakness," Mary-Kate admits. "It's gum. I'll stuff five pieces in my mouth if no one is looking!"

Having a successful clothing line was something the girls once only dreamed about. "We love fashion and thought a lot about having a clothing line when we got older," says Ashley. "And now it's really happening."

Over time the line has grown to include cosmetics, handbags, accessories, fragrances, shampoo, and sheets and duvets. In 2003 *mary-kateandashley* brand fashions spread around the globe. Now they are available in various stores in countries such as Australia, the United Kingdom and Mexico. And soon they'll be in other countries, too!

The *mary-kateandashley* Brand

Mary-Kate and Ashley are more than just teen actors and fashion designers. They continue to have a successful line of books based on characters they've played, and in 2001 were editors-in-chief of *mary-kateand-ashley* magazine. *mary-kateandashley* had a more grown-up look than other teen magazines. "We covered fashion, music, movies, sports, yoga and guys," says Mary-Kate. While the magazine was very popular, after three issues it was put on hold; the publishing company behind the magazine went out of business.

While they were disappointed about the hold on their magazine, the sisters have kept busy with other fun ventures, like their line of fashion dolls with Mattel. "It's a little weird to see yourself as a doll," admits Ashley.

In 2000, the fashion dolls looked like Mary-Kate and Ashley during their short-haired days of *TWO of a kind*. In 2002 Mattel introduced a Mary-Kate and Ashley Sweet 16 line of fashion dolls that have a more contemporary look and resemble the sisters with longer hair.

Then there's Mary-Kate and Ashley's popular line of interactive video games based on themselves. "We both thought creating video games for girls was a good idea," says Ashley. "Most video games are geared to boys, but these games are all about things girls like to do."

Their simple concept turned into a huge success. "We're happy that our fans like them," Mary-Kate says.

When the *Winners Circle* game was released, it quickly became the hottest-selling game among girls for both Game Boy and PlayStation2. The game featured the girls horseback riding.

From concept to actually playing the game once it's finished, Mary-Kate and Ashley are key advisers every step of the way. "We are involved in the whole process," says Ashley. "We're shown the game in different stages and we give our input."

Other Mary-Kate and Ashley video games have included *Magical Mystery Mall*, *The New Adventures of Mary-Kate and Ashley*, *Crush Course* and *Get a Clue*.

Sweet 16: Licenced to Drive is their most innovative video game so far. *Sweet 16: Licenced to Drive* invites kids to join Mary-Kate and Ashley for a huge birthday bash. The party games include a challenging driver's test, rock-climbing, jet-skiing, surfing, and many more things that Mary-Kate and Ashley like to do in real life!

With clothes, makeup, accessories, bedding, games

and much more, the *mary-kateandashley* brand is a hit! While it may sound like a job (and it is!), Mary-Kate and Ashley are having fun and are still the same down-to-earth girls they've always been. "It's kind of hard to even say that we are a brand," says Mary-Kate. "We don't think of ourselves like that. We're just us."

Chapter 8

Past, Present, Personal

On *Full House* Michelle once got into trouble at school when she accidentally let the class bird out of its cage. But by the end of the episode, she made up for it by replacing the bird.

Real life, though, can be a little more complicated! Mary-Kate and Ashley's home life is probably a lot like yours. They sometimes have school problems, questions about boys, worries about friends. And those kinds of problems are hardly ever solved as fast as they are on TV!

Like most teens, Mary-Kate and Ashley have to listen to their parents. They have curfews and rules that they need to follow.

Mary-Kate and Ashley's parents are careful not

to let the girls' careers get in the way of having a normal family and social life. The sisters still make plenty of time to see their friends – as long as their homework gets done. It's very important that Mary-Kate and Ashley keep up their grades, no matter how busy their careers. As they approach the end of high school, grades are particularly important. They need to earn the highest grades they can to get into a great college.

"Mary-Kate and Ashley are two of the most disciplined people I know," says a producer who works with them. "They are extremely focused. Not only do they learn their lines and deal with the other aspects of acting, but they study and do homework, too. They have an excellent work ethic, which allows them to get it all done – and done well."

Like any students, though, the sisters each have classes that aren't their favourites, but they still work hard at doing the very best they can.

"Ashley and Mary-Kate give over a hundred percent to everything they do," says their dad.

Mary-Kate and Ashley go to a great school. No one makes a big deal about their being celebrities or being twins. "When we're not working we go to regular classes like everybody else," says Ashley.

"We have lots of good friends at school. We are not treated any differently."

Still, just like everyone else, they sometimes get teased. "The only thing they give us a hard time about is being petite," reveals Mary-Kate, with a grin. "We're really little," Ashley adds. "Our brother Trent says it takes two of us just to make one person." As they wrapped up their junior year of high school, Ashley was five feet one inch, and Mary-Kate was five feet.

While they may seem cool and collected on screen, the one thing that does make them nervous is performing in front of a live audience. But they still want to talk to their fans, so they don't let the nervous jitters stop them.

At the age of seven they were already speaking to 3,000 kids and parents at Walt Disney World. Later, they talked to 20,000 fans at the Mall of America in Minneapolis! And more recently, they were award presenters at the live MTV Music Video Awards with thousands of fans and millions of television viewers around the world cheering them on.

Yes, they do a great job in front of crowds, but they still get butterflies in their stomachs – just like when you stand up in front of your class at school to give a speech.

Mary-Kate and Ashley don't have any problem at all making movies. If they need to film a scene over again, they do. It's all edited later and any mistakes the girls make get left out. But it's different when they appear on a talk show, like *The Tonight Show*. "You can't do it again if you mess up," says Mary-Kate. Through practice, though, the girls are getting over their fear of appearing live. "We do a lot of deep breathing beforehand," says Mary-Kate. "That usually helps."

As teens, the girls find new challenges to tackle such as taking their driver's tests, applying to colleges, and, of course, boys. Through school and friends, Mary-Kate and Ashley are meeting guys, and dating.

What kind of guy makes a good boyfriend? They both like independent guys who can think for themselves. "He has to be funny, cute and nice. And he can't whine a lot," says Mary-Kate. Ashley likes guys who are smart, driven and motivated, as well as "funny and cute – and not clingy!" Do we even need to mention that Ashley has to approve of the guys Mary-Kate wants to date, and vice versa? They do, of course!

For Mary-Kate and Ashley's sixteenth birthday, they went on a double date they would remember for the rest of their lives. They were taken to their favourite restaurant for dinner. What they didn't know was that inside would be eighty of their

1992

Mary-Kate: *"I want to be a candymaker and a cowgirl when I grow up."*

Ashley: *"I would like to be a candymaker and an actress. The food scenes are so much fun!"*

1994

Mary-Kate: *"I want to be an animal trainer for the movies. I want to have my own horse ranch."*

Ashley: *"I want to be a makeup artist, or I might keep acting."*

1997

Mary-Kate: *"I would like to train dolphins and whales, preferably at Sea World."*

Ashley: *"I really like acting. It's a lot of fun. And I would like to direct someday, too."*

2001

Mary-Kate: *"I see myself still acting, running our company and horseback riding."*

Ashley: *"I want to direct, but I also want to be really active in running our company and working with our fashion line."*

friends, family, and co-workers waiting to yell, "Surprise!" Their sweet sixteen party featured a photo booth, a Tarot card reader, dancing and a lot of fun! They each got a birthday cake decorated to look like a California driver's licence – complete with their pictures on it!

So far the guys they've dated haven't been in show business, but the girls do have show biz friends. Prince of pop Aaron Carter counts himself as one of their admirers. "I'll tell you the truth, I love the Olsen twins," Aaron admits.

As Ashley and Mary-Kate get older, they're beginning to develop a very sophisticated style. They've been photographed for many magazines – *Vogue*, *Vanity Fair*, *Women's Wear Daily* and *People*, to name a few of the hundreds they've been in.

So what's next? As they've grown up, Mary-Kate and Ashley's ideas about what they'd like to do in the future sure have changed. Now that the girls are teenagers, a whole new world of choices awaits them.

Will they go to college as planned?

Continue to act?

Move to careers behind the camera?

Continue to be fashion designers?

It's all possible! Mary-Kate and Ashley have

proved they are talented in show business, the fashion business *and* in school. There's no reason why they can't do it all!

The sisters are currently waiting to see which colleges accept them. They want to attend school together, preferably on the East Coast, which would be far from home but close to one of their favourite cities, New York City.

They will likely study both business and theatre. Ashley loves the business side of things while Mary-Kate leans towards the creative side. Mary-Kate is also interested in taking courses in photography and cooking. She will also keep up her riding while away at school. Both girls hope to spend a semester studying abroad, possibly in Italy.

Mary-Kate and Ashley are also working on a feature film for their own production company and Warner Bros. and are looking very carefully at how their movie characters are developed. The roles they want to play are a bit more grown-up. "We might want to try something a little more dramatic," Ashley says.

"But we wouldn't rule out an action movie," adds Mary-Kate. "Car chases. Stunts. Danger. That sounds like a lot of fun."

And there are people they would like to be able

to work with as well. "It would be great to work with Cameron Diaz or Luke Wilson," Mary-Kate says.

"I admire what Reese Witherspoon and Drew Barrymore are doing," Ashley adds. "They're on the big screen as actresses, and they're producing movies that they *don't* star in."

One thing the sisters may try some day is directing. Since they've grown up in front of a camera, they've learned the basics. They produce the movies they star in. "I can't wait to learn more about directing," Ashley says. "It's something I'd like to pursue in college."

For now, acting is still Ashley and Mary-Kate's number one interest. But if they want to give up acting and be everyday kids, that's okay. "If the girls ever decide they've had enough, that's fine," says their mom. "So far, that hasn't come close to happening."

"We would say 'We've had enough,'" Mary-Kate says, "if we wanted to quit." She turns to her sister and they both break into a big grin.

"But we're not going to say it because we love doing this," Ashley adds.

The phenomenal success of Mary-Kate and Ashley stems from familiarity. "Fans feel like they're close to us because they've seen us grow up," Mary-Kate tells us. But their popularity hasn't gone to their heads.

"There are fashion dolls of us and Game Boys of us, but it doesn't really faze us," says Ashley.

When asked about what accomplishments they'll be most proud of, Ashley says, "Staying grounded while all this is going on around us." Mary-Kate adds, "Graduating from high school and going to college."

And for the near future, the two will be working and playing together on screen and off. "Maybe in the future we'll do a movie or something separately," predicts Mary-Kate. Ashley chimes in, "One day when we're a lot older, but we have no idea when that will be. Right now, we're going to have fun *together!*"

Mary-Kate and Ashley have hopes and dreams just like you. Many of their dreams are coming true. And they know how it can happen for you, too!

"If you really want to do something, go for it," advises Ashley. "Work hard and you will succeed."

MARY-KATE AND ASHLEY
FUN FACTS

• When *Full House* began, Mary-Kate's name was *not* hyphenated.

• In photographs where the girls are dressed in blue and pink or red, it's almost always Mary-Kate wearing blue and Ashley in pink or red.

• In 1993 they were Junior Grand Marshals of the holiday Christmas parade in Hollywood.

• They've made movies in the United States, England, Australia, the Bahamas, Mexico, France, and Canada.

• Mary-Kate and Ashley rode on the Jell-O float in the 1997 Macy's Thanksgiving Day Parade.

• The sisters have been guests of honour on six Sail With The Stars cruises including ones to Russia, the Carribean and Alaska.

• Mary-Kate and Ashley were named Teen Ambassadors to the U.S. Women's World Cup soccer team in 1999, the year the team won!

• The sisters both like to fall asleep with their televisions on.

• They've starred in four television series: *Full House, TWO of a kind, So Little Time,* and *Mary-Kate and Ashley in ACTION!*

• Nickelodeon viewers voted them the Best Female Actresses of the Year for the film *It Takes Two* in 1996.

• They won this award again in 1998 for their roles as Mary-Kate and Ashley Burke on *TWO of a kind*.

• The girls played themselves in a 1998 episode of the soap opera *All My Children* and appeared as guest stars in an episode of *7th Heaven* in 2000.

• Mary-Kate was honoured with a Daytime Emmy nomination in 2002 for her role in *So Little Time*.

• They received the first ever DVD Premiere Franchise Performers Award in 2003 for their phenomenal success in the DVD market.

• Throughout their careers, Mary-Kate and Ashley have been featured in more than 100,000 newspaper stories, they have been on the cover of dozens of magazines around the world, and they have appeared over 100 times on TV talk shows and programs like NBC's *Today* and *The Tonight Show with Jay Leno*.

MARY-KATE

FULL NAME: Mary-Kate Olsen (no middle name)

BIRTHDATE: June 13, 1986 (about two minutes after Ashley)

HAIR COLOUR: Blonde

EYE COLOUR: Blue-green

FEATURES: Left-handed
One inch shorter than Ashley
A freckle on her right cheek
Rounder face

FAVOURITE HOBBIES: Horseback riding, yoga

FAVOURITE SHOES: "Sandals, but we call them flip-flops."

FAVOURITE STORES: Boutiques in Los Angeles and New York City and Rome

FAVOURITE CLOTHING: Watches, funky necklaces, blue jeans, T-shirts, cashmere sweaters

FAVOURITE TELEVISION SHOWS: *Will & Grace*, *Friends*

FAVOURITE MOVIE: *Best in Show*

FAVOURITE KIND OF BOOKS: Real life books, no fantasy

FAVOURITE ACTORS: Cameron Diaz and Drew Barrymore

CELEBRITY CRUSH: Luke Wilson

FAVOURITE SCHOOL SUBJECT: Creative writing
LEAST FAVOURITE SCHOOL SUBJECT: Maths
PICK A NUMBER: 8
WHAT'S IN HER BAG: Lip gloss, gum, wallet, mobile phone
FAVOURITE SPORTS: Basketball and hockey
FAVOURITE EXERCISE: Yoga
FAVOURITE ANIMAL: Horse
COLLECTS: Candles
SATURDAY NIGHT ROUTINE: Dinner and a movie with friends
RISE AND SHINE: "I like to wake up early!"
DRINK OF CHOICE: Ice-blended mocha
FAVOURITE FOOD: Sushi
FAVOURITE VEGGIE: Broccoli
FAVOURITE ICE CREAM: Mocha
FAVOURITE GUM FLAVOUR: Strawberry
FAVOURITE COLOURS: Maroon and blue
HOLIDAY OF CHOICE: Christmas
DESCRIBE YOURSELF: "Outgoing."
IN THE FUTURE: "I see myself going to college, acting in and producing feature films, and continuing to run our company."

ASHLEY

FULL NAME: Ashley Fuller Olsen (Fuller is her mom's maiden name)

BIRTHDATE: June 13, 1986 (about two minutes before Mary-Kate)

HAIR COLOUR: Blonde

EYE COLOUR: Blue-green

FEATURES: Right-handed
An inch taller than Mary-Kate
Oval face

FAVOURITE HOBBIES: Yoga and golf

FAVOURITE SHOES: Flip-flops

FAVOURITE STORES: Boutiques in Los Angeles, New York City and Rome

FAVOURITE CLOTHING: Accessories, accessories, accessories

FAVOURITE TELEVISION SHOWS: *Will & Grace*, *Friends*

FAVOURITE MOVIE: *Waiting for Guffman*

FAVOURITE KIND OF BOOKS: Mysteries and historical fiction

FAVOURITE ACTORS: Julia Roberts and Drew Barrymore

CELEBRITY CRUSH: Ben Affleck

FAVOURITE SCHOOL SUBJECT: Maths

LEAST FAVOURITE SCHOOL SUBJECT: English

AFTER-SCHOOL ACTIVITIES: Yoga, homework, hanging out with friends

PICK A NUMBER: 8

WHAT'S IN HER BAG: Lip gloss, mobile phone, wallet, and day planner

FAVOURITE SPORTS: Football and hockey

FAVOURITE EXERCISE: Pilates (at the moment)

COLLECTS: Music

SATURDAY NIGHT ROUTINE: Dinner and hanging out with friends

RISE AND SHINE: "I like to sleep in!"

DRINK OF CHOICE: Chai tea latte

FAVOURITE FOODS: Angel hair pasta with tomato and basil sauce, sushi

FAVORITE VEGGIE: Broccoli

FAVORITE ICE CREAM: Cookie Dough

FAVOURITE COLOURS: Yellow, purple, and blue

HOLIDAY OF CHOICE: Christmas

DESCRIBE YOURSELF: "Organised, loyal and fun."

IN THE FUTURE: "I see myself going to college, acting in and producing feature films, and continuing to run our company."

Get the latest on Mary-Kate and Ashley on their official website, *marykateandashley.com!*

And while you're at it, send them an e-mail, too.

Don't forget to ask your parents' permission before you log on!

ABOUT THE AUTHOR

Damon Romine is an entertainment journalist. He has co-authored a series of *Life Stories* books on Britney Spears, 'N SYNC, the Backstreet Boys, Ricky Martin, Leonardo DiCaprio, Matt Damon, the Spice Girls and *Dawson's Creek*. A founding editor of the teen magazine *J-14*, Damon has also served as the editor of the magazines *Tiger Beat*, *Teen Beat* and *Teen*. He lives in Los Angeles with his beagle, Abby.

PSSST! Take a sneak peak at

It's a Twin Thing

"Twenty hours to go," Mary-Kate Burke reported as she rode up the escalator at the mall. Checking her calendar watch, she wished it was fast – a whole month fast!

Her twin sister, Ashley, tapped her on the shoulder. "Did you say something, Mary-Kate?"

"Our hours of freedom are numbered," Mary-Kate declared. "Doesn't that mean anything to you?"

Ashley blew her blonde fringe out of her eyes. "Mary-Kate, it's just the last day of summer vacation. Not the end of the world."

"Oh, yeah? Well, it is for me," Mary-Kate grumbled. "I am not looking forward to seventh grade! Especially with Miss Tandy. I hear she's the toughest teacher in the whole city of Chicago!"

She glanced over her shoulder at her father, Kevin Burke, who stood a few steps behind them on the escalator.

"Okay, girls," Kevin said as they reached the top. "We had our frozen yogurts and chicken fajitas. Now you have exactly one hour to find your back-to-school outfits."

"How about a prison uniform?" Mary-Kate muttered.

"Nah," Ashley said. She looked Mary-Kate up and down. "Orange isn't your colour."

"Ha, ha." Mary-Kate tugged at her oversize T-shirt. She hated going shopping. Unless it was for baseball caps, knee pads, sneakers . . .

"Here it is," Ashley gushed as they entered Bailey's department store. They walked into a section filled with skinny black jeans, colourful sweaters, and T-shirts. "My idea of paradise – the girls' department!"

Mary-Kate groaned when she saw all the signs that read BACK TO SCHOOL. Talk about in-your-face!

"Hey, girls," Kevin said. He held up a pink dress with big blue dots and a white collar. "How about this nifty number?"

Mary-Kate rolled her eyes. She might not be interested in fashion, but even she could tell that her dad's taste in clothes was . . . well, a little behind the times.

"Dad, please," Ashley whispered. She glanced around to make sure no one was looking. "We're eleven years old. We're going into the seventh grade. Not pre-school."

"Yeah," Mary-Kate agreed. "Think of our reputations."

Kevin shrugged as he hung the pink dress back on the rack. "Girls wore this when I was in seventh grade."

"They also had dinosaurs for pets," Mary-Kate shot back.

Kevin shook his head. "Impossible. The dinosaur became extinct ages before man first appeared— "

"Uh-oh." Ashley sighed. "Lecture number five thousand and fifty-three."

Mary-Kate grinned. "What else is new?" Having a college professor for a dad meant a lot of lectures. Lectures during breakfast, dinner, a drive – even while taking out the trash!

"Dad." Ashley interrupted their father, who was still talking about dinosaurs. She pointed to a row of chairs next to the elevators. "Why don't you have a seat with the other bored dads while Mary-Kate and I try on clothes?"

"It's a deal," Kevin said. He pressed his palms together. "But please – only one outfit apiece. I'm still paying the credit card bill from the last time you two went shopping."

"Calm down, Dad," Mary-Kate said. "I just need a new pair of jeans. And maybe some new studs for my baseball sneakers."

"Speak for yourself," Ashley said. She waited until Kevin was out of the way. Then she grabbed Mary-Kate's arm.

"All systems go," she whispered. "We'll start with sportswear and work our way up to party clothes – just in case we're really popular this year!"

Sighing, Mary-Kate watched Ashley trot towards a table piled with sweaters. Her neat white shorts and cotton cardigan said it all – when it came to clothes, Ashley meant business!

"Which do you like better?" Ashley called as she held up two sweaters. "The grey or the red? I think the grey might bring out our blue eyes better – but this red looks great with blonde hair."

"I don't care. I'll take whichever one doesn't itch," Mary-Kate said, joining her sister at the sweater table.

Ashley rolled her eyes. "How can we be twins and have such totally different tastes?" she demanded.

"Well, we're not identical twins," Mary-Kate pointed out. "Even though most people have trouble telling us apart."

Ashley tossed the sweaters back on the table.

"Why am I the only one in this family who loves to shop?"

"Mom loved to shop," Mary-Kate said. "Remember?"

A slow, sad smile spread across Ashley's face. "Yeah. Mom used to say that if she had just one day to live, she'd spend it at the mall."

Mary-Kate chuckled, but deep inside she felt sad, too.

Their mom didn't spend her last day at the mall. She spent it in the hospital. The twins were just eight years old when she died – but Mary-Kate remembered every detail as if it happened only yesterday.

"Mom was so much fun," Mary-Kate said. "I really miss her."

"So do I," Ashley said. "Dad is great – but he's not a mom."

Mary-Kate nodded. Since their mom died, Kevin had tried hard to be both mother and father to them. In fact, sometimes he tried too hard!

Ashley had gone back to picking sweaters. Mary-

Kate stared. The pile in Ashley's arms almost reached her chin!

"Okay," Ashley called. "I'm all set. What are you going to try on, Mary-Kate?"

"I want an oversize jersey with a Cubs emblem on it," Mary-Kate decided.

"I don't see any of those around," Ashley said.

"That's because they're not in this section," Mary-Kate said. "They're in the boys' department. Let's go."

"The boys' department?" Ashley gasped. "You can't!"

"Why not?" Mary-Kate demanded. She hurried towards the other end of the floor. "Just because I'm a girl doesn't mean I have to dress like a total princess."

"Mary-Kate, wait!" Ashley called. "Don't go into the boys' dressing room... And I do not dress like a princess!"

Mary-Kate glanced over her shoulder and laughed. Ashley was trying to balance the tower of sweaters as she ran after her.

When Mary-Kate reached the boys' department, she spotted two boys from her school: Michael Cruz and a kid with light brown hair. He has some weird nickname, Mary-Kate thought. Something like Hokey . . . or Dopey . . . or . . .

Ashley ran up behind her, out of breath.

"Pokey," Mary-Kate remembered out loud.

"Pokey Valentine."

Ashley gasped. "What?"

"That kid over there by the socks," Mary-Kate explained. "Pokey Valentine. He's in our class this year."

Ashley's head snapped to the side. She peered at Pokey. Then she ducked behind her pile of sweaters. Her cheeks turned red.

"Pokey Valentine? Oh, wow!" she whispered.

Mary-Kate stared at her sister. "What's with you? Why are you acting like such a weirdo?"

"I'm not!" Ashley protested.

"Whatever." Mary-Kate picked up a baseball cap. As she tried it on, she felt Ashley jab her in the shoulder with one finger.

"Are you sure Pokey Valentine is in our class this year?" Ashley asked quietly. "Who told you? How do you know?"

"I saw him at a baseball game this summer," Mary-Kate explained. "He said he has Miss Tandy – just like we do."

Ashley shoved the pile of sweaters into Mary-Kate's arms. Then she spun around and started hurrying towards the escalator. "Wait. *Now* where are you going?" Mary-Kate called.

"I just remembered some stuff I have to buy," Ashley said.

"What stuff?" Mary-Kate asked.

Ashley stopped and glanced over her shoulder. "You know – lipstick, eye shadow, blusher."

"You mean *make-up?*" Mary-Kate shrieked.

"Shh!" Ashley hissed. She darted a glance at Pokey Valentine. "Not so loud. He'll hear you!"

Then Mary-Kate got it.

"Oh, no," she groaned. She pulled the baseball cap down over her eyes. "Ashley's got a crush!"

so little time

Check out book 1!

how to train a boy

"**H**urry up, Riley!" fourteen-year-old Chloe Carlson called to her sister. "I need to do my hair."

"I'll be out in a second!" Riley called back from the bathroom.

Chloe kept staring intently out of the window of the bedroom she shared with Riley. Left was the street. Right was the beach. She gave each view a three-second scan. Pavement on the left. Sand on the right.

Nobody in sight.

The bathroom door opened, and Chloe's sister came into the bedroom. Riley's shoulder-length blonde hair was wet from the shower. Chloe's longer blonde hair was covered with soft curlers.

"Here I am," Riley announced, wrapping a towel around her head. "How's the boywatch going?"

"No one so far," Chloe replied. She'd come up with the idea of a before-school boywatch last week, on the first day of school. That was the first time she'd ever seen Travis Morgan.

She'd been standing in the exact same place when she spotted him down on the beach. She didn't know his name then, of course. But she thought he looked really cute. Short brown hair, long tanned legs. She'd watched as he climbed the stairs to the street and disappeared from sight.

Then, that same day, she'd seen him at West Malibu High, where she and Riley had just started as freshmen. And he wasn't just cute, he was hot.

Thanks to her friend Tara Jordan's older brother, Chloe now knew Travis's name. She also knew he was a junior, and that he didn't have a girlfriend (yet). What she didn't know was Travis himself.

"He has to walk by again *some* time," she murmured, still staring out the window.

"Sure he does," Riley agreed. "Didn't Tara's brother say he was having trouble with his dirt bike?"

Chloe nodded. That was another thing she'd learned about Travis – he had a dirt bike, and he hung out with some other guys who had them, too. They all had a reputation for cutting classes and getting detention.

[**Chloe**: I know, I know. You're thinking, "Stay

away from this guy, Chloe. Detention, dirt bikes...definitely bad news." But you wouldn't be saying that if you'd met Travis. Okay, well, I haven't exactly met him, either, but there's no way a boy that cute could be bad news. I'm telling you, I know about these things. Or at least I'm willing to find out.]

Chloe crossed her fingers, hoping that Travis would have major trouble with his bike. Then when he walked by again, she could "bump" into him.

"If I can just get a chance to talk to him, I'm sure I can make him like me," she said to Riley. "I've passed him in the hall three times this week, but he hardly notices me."

"Probably because you're a freshman," Riley said, taking some clothes out of the wardrobe. "It's like we're marked."

"I know," Chloe agreed. "That's why I need to get into a conversation with him. Today I'm going to try to find out where his locker is."

"Then what?" Riley asked.

"I'll play lost and ask directions to the science wing or someplace."

"Bad idea," Riley advised. "I mean, this is Friday, right? We started school last Wednesday. If you don't know where the science wing is by now, Travis will think you're totally clueless."

"Good point," Chloe agreed, trying to think of

something else she could ask Travis.

Riley finished changing into jeans and a peach-coloured top. "Okay, my turn at the window."

As soon as Riley took her place, Chloe hurried to the dressing table across the room. "At least the boywatch isn't a total loss," Chloe said, taking the rollers from her hair. "I haven't seen Larry, either."

"You mean you haven't seen him *yet*," Riley told her.

"True," Chloe admitted. Larry Slotnick, their next-door neighbour, almost always managed to show up. He'd had a crush on Riley since first grade, and no matter how many times Riley turned him down, he still kept asking her out.

"I've been thinking," Chloe said as she brushed her hair. "You know what your problem is, Riley?"

[**Riley:** Okay, here's the thing – even though Chloe and I are both fourteen, she was born eight minutes earlier. That makes her my 'older' sister, so she likes giving me advice.]

"What's my problem?" Riley asked. She picked up the towel and began briskly rubbing her hair. She wore hers straight and didn't need quite as much mirror time.

"Well, for one thing, you shouldn't dry your hair like that," Chloe said. "It'll get all snarled and then you'll have split ends."

"That's my problem – split ends?" Riley asked.

"It will be if you're not careful." Chloe opened her jewellery box and took out a pair of blue enamelled earrings to go with the blue top she was wearing. "You're supposed to just squeeze your hair with the towel."

Riley started squeezing her hair.

"Your other problem is boys," Chloe said, putting the earrings in her ears. "You're way too picky."

Riley stared at her.

"Keep watching out of the window!" Chloe cried. "It takes only fifteen seconds for somebody to walk by. I timed it."

"Wait – back up to my problem with boys," Riley said, turning to the window again. "Don't tell me you think I should go out with Larry."

"Well, no," Chloe admitted.

"Good." Riley breathed a sigh of relief. "Because I like Larry, but not that way. He's a friend – a very goofy friend. We've known him forever, remember?"

"Yes, but forget about Larry," Chloe said. "The problem is, you're always getting crushes on actors and rock stars. They seem perfect and you know why? Because they're not real."

"They're not?" Riley asked. "Whoa, has anybody told them? Does Brad Pitt know he's not real?"

Chloe laughed. "You know what I mean. They're

fantasy guys. Real boys have rough edges. You sort of have to mould them. But at least you have a chance with them."

"Like you have with Travis, you mean."

"Exactly," Chloe agreed. "Just because Travis hasn't noticed me yet doesn't mean he never will. Travis is *possible*, see? I just have to find a way to make it happen."

Checking her hair again, Chloe tried to think of other ways to make it happen with Travis. Once she learned where his locker was, she and her friends could hang out around there before homeroom. Maybe she'd try to find out his class schedule, too, so she'd have maximum opportunities to meet him.

A rap on the door interrupted Chloe's thoughts. She glanced up as her mother hurried into the room.

Macy Carlson was slender, with brown hair and eyes and a habit of speaking quickly, especially when she was nervous or under pressure. "What do you think?" she asked, holding out an armful of filmy material dotted with tiny jet beads and rhinestones.

"It's gorgeous. Is that for the MTV dress?" Chloe asked. The MTV awards would be broadcast in less than two weeks, and their mother had been hired to design a dress for a model named Tedi. Tedi was going to present an award. That meant Mom's dress

would be seen by millions of people. Needless to say, it was a big deal.

Mrs. Carlson nodded. "It's going to be ankle-length, and I'm thinking scalloped hemline, maybe higher in front, but not knee-high, that would be too Flamenco dancer, I just want a nice swirly effect so the beads and rhinestones will catch the light," she said without taking a breath.

"Slow down, Mom," Riley told her.

"And calm down," Chloe added.

"Not possible," Macy said. "This is the first dress I've designed on my own since your dad left the business, and it has to be an absolute knock-out." She rushed out of the door, then popped her head back in. "See you two later. Love you!"

"Love you, too, Mom," Chloe called. She turned to Riley. "Mom's really hyper today."

"She's always been hyper," Riley said as their mother's footsteps clattered down the hall. "Now she's practically a wreck."

"Um-hmm," Chloe agreed, applying some lip gloss. It had been several months since their parents decided to have a trial separation. Before that, they'd run a fashion-design business together. Now their mother was running it on her own. Chloe knew she could do it, but it was sort of like living with a whirlwind.

Their dad, on the other hand, was so calm, he

was almost asleep. He hadn't taken another job yet, but he wasn't worried since he had plenty of investments. He'd just bought a house trailer to live in on a bluff overlooking the beach.

"What do you think Dad's new place will be like?" Chloe asked. She and Riley were going to see it for the first time today after school.

Riley turned to face Chloe. "When I talked to him yesterday, he said it's perfect for him," Riley replied. "Small and simple. That's what he wanted, remember? A simpler life."

"I guess you can't get much simpler than a single-wide trailer," Chloe agreed. As she leaned towards the mirror for a final inspection, she saw a face pop up in the window – spiky brown hair, close-together eyes, a big mouth, and a goofy, hopeful expression.

Larry Slotnick's face.

Larry's head stayed visible for approximately two seconds, then disappeared.

"Riley," Chloe said.

"I saw him. Did you leave the trampoline out again?" Riley asked accusingly.

"Oops." Chloe grinned. "Sorry. Ignore him. Maybe he'll go away."

"It's Larry," Riley reminded her. "He never goes away."

Larry's face bounced back into the window

frame. "Riley!" he called. "Will you..." He disappeared again.

Riley hung her towel over the wardrobe doorknob and joined Chloe at the dressing table.

Larry bounced into view. "Riley, will you go out with me?" he asked quickly.

"No." Riley began combing her still-damp hair.

Larry disappeared and bounced up again. This time he grabbed hold of the window ledge and clung to it. "Give me one good reason why not," he said.

Riley glanced at his reflection in the mirror. "Because you're hanging from my window?" she asked with a grin.

"Okay, you have a point," Larry agreed. "But, Riley, I can't help myself. You're the only thing in the world I need to be happy. Just you."

Chloe turned around. "That's it?" she asked him. "Just Riley?"

Larry thought for a second. "Well, and maybe my PlayStation Two. But that's it," he added quickly. "Just Riley and my PlayStation Two. That's all I'll ever need." He paused. "And maybe a breakfast burrito."

Riley couldn't help laughing as she crossed the room and picked up her backpack.

"So is it okay if I hang for a while?" Larry asked. "Just make believe I'm not here."

104

Riley slung her pack over her shoulder, gave Chloe and Larry a little wave, and headed out of the door.

Chloe walked over to the window. She couldn't help feeling a little sympathy for Larry. After all, they were both trying to attract someone.

Of course, that was absolutely all they had in common. As she'd told Riley, Travis was possible. She had a chance with him. But for Larry, Riley was definitely not possible.

"Hey, Chloe, do you think Riley's coming back?" Larry asked.

"I guess she'll have to, eventually." Chloe took one more glance out of the window and gasped.

"What?" Startled, Larry tightened his grip on the window ledge. "What's wrong?"

"Nothing. Just slide over — quick!" Chloe told him. She had just spotted a boy in the distance, walking along the beach. Was it Travis?

"Actually, I think I'll just hop down and head to school," Larry said.

As Larry dropped down to the trampoline, Chloe peered out of the window at the boy. He was farther away than when Chloe had seen him last week. She squinted, trying to bring him into focus.

Jeans and a black T-shirt. Brown hair? Yes, definitely. But was it him?

The guy still wasn't close enough for her to see

any more details. But Chloe wasn't waiting any longer. She grabbed her bookbag and rushed from the room. If it *was* Travis, this could be her big chance!

to be continued...

Sweet 16

Book 1:
NEVER BEEN KISSED

"Ashley? Are you ready yet?" I called out, barely able to hide the excitement in my voice.

"Just give me a couple of minutes!" my sister, Ashley, answered from the dressing room next to mine.

I stared at myself in the mirror. The store dressing room was completely littered with clothes, but I'd found the perfect outfit at last. I couldn't stop smiling. "Do I look great or what?" I asked myself.

The answer was yes.

The knit top I'd chosen brought out my blue eyes and looked killer with the short denim shorts. It was perfect for our sweet sixteen party.

"Ashley, hurry up!" I called. "I'm dying to see what you think of this outfit!"

"I've just got a few more dresses to try," Ashley called back. I rolled my eyes and sat down to wait on the little bench in my dressing room, pushing

the pile of clothes aside. *Our party is going to be sooo great*, I thought. I let my mind wander off...

All of our girlfriends are hanging out on the beach and it's a sunny, breezy day. There's a DJ spinning in the sand while a bunch of people dance to the latest songs. A few people swim in the waves. The rest of the crowd watches as Ashley and I rule in a volleyball tournament. Dad mans the barbecue while Mom snaps pictures of our friends.

We hang out on the beach until the stars come out, dancing to our favourite hits next to a big bonfire. Our cake is huge and has tons of candles on it. All our friends gather around to sing to us. Everyone agrees that it's the most fantastic sweet sixteen they've ever been to.

And of course, there's a monster pile of presents waiting for us when it's all over. Can't forget about the presents...

"Almost ready, Mary-Kate." Ashley's voice snapped me out of my thoughts. The beach and the party all melted away. "Just give me two more minutes."

"No problem," I told her, smiling at my reflection in the dressing room mirror. After all, I could spend another half-hour just daydreaming about the presents!

Okay, Ashley, I said to myself, *you saved the*

best dress for last. Time to go for it.

I hung up all the outfits I'd already tried on.
Then I turned and took the last dress down from
the hook on the back of the door. I had a feeling
that this was going to be *the one*.

I slipped the long, flowy, light-blue gown over my
head, and it fell perfectly on my frame. The dress
looked like it was made for me – it was
just the right length, fitted perfectly around the waist
and its slim spaghetti straps were totally flattering.
Plus, it sparkled when the light hit it just right.

Mary-Kate is going to love this so much, I
thought. *She's going to want to get the exact same
dress!*

I gathered up my long, wavy blonde hair into a
twist and secured it with a clip. Then I stood up on
my tiptoes and grinned at my reflection.
I'd found it! The perfect outfit for our sweet
sixteen...

*Mary-Kate and I walk into a huge ballroom filled
with people who are all dressed up in ball gowns
and tuxedos. Elegantly dressed waiters circle the
room carrying trays heaped with food and tall
champagne glasses full of sparkling cider. The scent
of flowers fills the air, and there are roses on
every table. Hundreds of candles give the room a
romantic glow.*

The dance floor gleams, and two incredibly cute guys ask me and Mary-Kate to dance. Mom and Dad stand along the wall, watching us with proud smiles. One of the waiters wheels out a huge cake, and everyone sings to us. When we blow out the candles, the whole room bursts into applause.

It's the most amazing party anyone has ever attended.

I shook myself out of my daydream and smiled at my reflection once again. It was all coming together. *Our sixteenth birthday is less than two months away*, I thought, *and now I've found the perfect dress – an elegant dress that shows I'm not a kid any more.*

"Ashley!" My sister groaned.

"Okay, I'm ready!" I stood and smoothed the dress once more. "Let's both come out on the count of three."

"Right," Mary-Kate said. "Here goes. One..."

"Two..." I chimed in.

"Three!"

We both stepped out of our dressing rooms, took one look at each other and burst out laughing.

"Um... I think we may have a problem here," I said, taking in her shorts and tank top.

"Tell me about it, Cinderella," she joked. "Nice dress, though."

"Thanks, and those shorts are great. But…" I shuffled over to her dressing room and peeked inside, taking in the piles of casual clothes. There wasn't a single dress in sight. "Mary-Kate, what were you thinking?"

"Beach party, of course!" she replied.

"But…we live in Malibu, California," I said. "We go to the beach all the time."

"Exactly," she said. "What's the point of living here if you don't take advantage of it?"

I took in her shorts and tank top again. When it came to our birthday party, we were definitely not on the same planet. "Maybe we should go somewhere and start talking about this party," I suggested.

Ashley and I kicked back in the cushy corner booth at Starbucks with our coffees. "We've got to get serious about this sweet sixteen party," she said. "I know you like to be spontaneous, but—"

"Hey," I protested. "Even I know that great parties take planning. Give me a *little* credit, Miss Organisation."

She pulled out a glittery purple notebook and matching pen. "I'm no more organised than the average person," she insisted.

"Does the average person alphabetise all the books in her bedroom?" I asked. "Does the average person keep all of her drawers colour

coordinated? I don't think so."

"All right," she said, sniffing. "So I'm above average. I just can't live in total chaos – like *some* people I know."

"Hey," I protested. "I don't live in chaos. I just...go with the flow." Though I have to admit the floor of my room is littered with shoes and I'm always tripping over them.

"Whatever." She tapped her purple pen, ready to work. "Back to the party. Where do we start?"

I zipped up the front of my dark blue hoodie and leaned my elbows on the table. "We've already been to a lot of sweet sixteens. Remember those goody bags from Sherra Cintron's party? With the CDs and the little disposable cameras? Those were cool."

"Yes! That *was* a good idea," Ashley agreed, making a note. "We could give out goody bags, too – something that goes along with our theme."

"Theme?" I flopped back against the velvety couch. "How are we supposed to find a theme that's got you wearing a ball gown and me hanging out in shorts and a T-shirt?"

"Okay, don't freak," Ashley said. "We'll just have to compromise, somehow."

"I know." I stirred my frappuccino with my straw. "I just wish we weren't born so late in the year. It's like there's all this pressure to top the parties that came before ours."

Ashley smiled confidently. "Hey, this is *our* party," she said. "It'll blow all those other ones out of the water." She glanced down at her notebook. "Who should we invite?"

"I've been thinking a lot about this," I said, sitting up again. "I think it should be an all-girl party."

"Really?" Ashley asked.

"Yeah. None of our friends has a serious boyfriend," I pointed out. "And I think everyone would have a lot more fun if they weren't worried about looking cool in front of the guys."

Ashley frowned. "I see your point. But we *are* turning sixteen. Wouldn't it be kind of...I don't know...unsophisticated to have an all-girl party?"

"Having guys there won't make it sophisticated," I said. "Most of our guy friends still think burping contests rule."

Ashley giggled. Then a movement by the door caught her eye. "Hey, there's Lauren and Brittany!"

Sure enough, our two best friends were making their way over to our table. Lauren and Brittany couldn't be more different if they tried. Lauren is tall with wavy brown hair, light skin and tons of freckles. She's always sweet to everyone and has an eternally sunny outlook. Brittany, on the other hand, can be sarcastic about anything – from breakfast cereal to biology class. She's African-

American and has dark brown eyes and tight black curls that she never lets grow past her earlobes.

Brittany waved to us. "Mary-Kate and Ashley – at Starbucks? What a shocker!"

"Hey, I'm not the one with the frequent-customer card," I shot back.

Lauren glanced down at Ashley's notebook.

"Gift bags?" she read. "For what?"

"We're trying to plan our sweet sixteen." Ashley sighed. "Unfortunately we haven't got very far."

"Ashley's thinking royal ball while I'm thinking beach party," I explained. "I picked out shorts and she picked out a dress...and she wants to invite the guys and I think it should be just girls."

Brittany laughed and shook her head, her dangly earrings jingling.

"Another shocker!" she joked. "Anyone who knows you two could have seen this coming."

"Are we that predictable?" Ashley asked.

"Kind of – in a good way," Lauren said. "But whatever you guys decide to do, I'm sure it'll be the best party ever. Everyone's already looking forward to it. I overheard Rachel and Alex talking about it the other day. They can't wait to see what you're going to do."

"No pressure or anything," Brittany cracked.

Pressure? I wasn't worried. A wave of calm washed over me.

Working together, Ashley and I would plan a sweet sixteen to end all sweet sixteens – I felt sure of it.

"Hey, we love pressure," I declared, leaning back into the couch. "We *live* for pressure."

"Okay, let's talk about themes." Ashley flipped her notebook to a new page. "What were some good ones from parties we've gone to?"

Lauren's blue eyes brightened. "I loved the Paris theme at Melanie Han's party, with the Eiffel Tower replica and all the twinkling lights."

"Okay, so something international would be good," Ashley said, making a note. "What else?"

"Hey! What about a Broadway theme?" Brittany suggested. "Ashley loves acting, and you could have a city skyline and playbills and stuff like that."

"Good one!" Ashley said, writing it down.

"Or we could do a Hollywood thing," I added, ideas starting to flit through my head. "We could have a replica of the Hollywood sign, a red carpet—"

"Or what about a Hawaiian theme!" Ashley chimed in. "Hula skirts, leis, coconuts, sand…"

"Or we could do a music theme—"

"Or Mardi Gras—"

"Guys!" Brittany cried, holding up her hands.

115

The rest of us stopped our babble fest. "Look who just walked in," she whispered.

I looked up, and my breath caught in my throat. Jake Impenna was headed for the coffee counter. Jake is an incredibly cute seventeen-year-old junior who just moved to Malibu a few months ago. His brown, spiky hair was hidden beneath a well-worn baseball cap, and he was wearing a grey T-shirt that matched his amazing eyes.

Jake was on the basketball and baseball teams at our school, Bayside High, and everyone saw him as this total jock. But he was also in my creative writing class, and I could tell from his stories that he had a seriously sensitive side. I had a monster crush on him, and my friends knew it. I felt their eyes on me while I stared at him.

"Are you gonna talk to him?" Brittany asked.

I blushed. "I don't feel like making an idiot of myself today."

Brittany raised her eyebrows. "Since when do you have trouble talking to anyone?"

"Since whenever Jake walks into a room," I answered. "I need at least half an hour to practise before I can even say hello to him."

"Well, start practising," Ashley said.

My heart raced and my mouth went dry. Jake was weaving through the café with his coffee... and heading right for our table!

mary-kateandashley

TWO of a kind ™

Coming soon – can you collect them all?

HarperCollins*Entertainment*

PARACHUTE PRESS

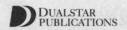

DUALSTAR PUBLICATIONS

AOL

mary-kateandashley.com
AOL Keyword: mary-kateandashley

mary-kateandashley

Mary-Kate & Ashley: Our Story
Meet Chloe and Riley Carlson.

So much to do...

so little time

... and more to come!

HarperCollins*Entertainment*

 PARACHUTE PRESS

 DUALSTAR PUBLICATIONS

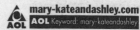 AOL mary-kateandashley.com
AOL Keyword: mary-kateandashley

TM & © 2002 Dualstar Entertainment Group, LLC.

mary-kateandashley

Sweet 16

(1) *Never Been Kissed*   (0 00 714879 8)
(2) *Wishes and Dreams*   (0 00 714880 1)
(3) *The Perfect Summer*   (0 00 714881 X)

HarperCollins*Entertainment*

PARACHUTE PRESS

DUALSTAR PUBLICATIONS

mary-kateandashley.com
AOL Keyword: mary-kateandashley

mary-kateandashley

Read the books from the hit movie 'New York Minute'.
Order **NOW** for **FREE** postage and packing! (*quote order code)

New York Minute   £4.99   0-00-718319-4

Mary-Kate and Ashley play twins Jane and Roxy Ryan who end up being chased all the way from Chinatown to Harlem by police, politicians and one angry truant officer... all in a New York Minute? With exclusive behind-the-scenes colour photos from the movie.

New York Minute — There's Something About Roxy   £4.99   0-00-718318-6

Starring Mary-Kate and Ashley as Jane and Roxy Ryan, characters from the hit movie! Roxy gets a hot job on a music video goes on an exciting road trip and finds her the romance of her life! Plus exciting movie pictures!

New York Minute — The Secret of Jane's Success   £4.99   0-00-718317-8

Things are cool until Jane Ryan uncovers a scandal, falls in love with her presidential opponent and, thanks to her wild sister, Roxy, ends up in jail. Read all about Mary-Kate and Ashley as Jane and Roxy Ryan — with behind-the-scenes movie photos!

To order by credit or debit card
just ask an adult to call 0870 787 1724 quoting order code 62Y.

™ & © 2004 Dualstar Entertainment Group, LLC.

HarperCollins*Entertainment*

PARACHUTE PRESS

DUALSTAR PUBLICATIONS

AOL **mary-kateandashley.co**
AOL Keyword: mary-kateandashl